PARADISE AS A GARDEN

**World
Landscape
Art &
Architecture
Series**

PARADISE AS A GARDEN

In Persia
and Mughal India

Elizabeth B. Moynihan

George Braziller
New York

**World
Landscape
Art &
Architecture
Series**

General Editor
WILLIAM HOWARD ADAMS

For information address the publisher:
George Braziller, Inc.
One Park Avenue
New York, N.Y. 10016

Library of Congress Cataloging in Publication Data

Moynihan, Elizabeth B.
   Paradise As A Garden In Persia and Mughal India.

   (World landscape art and architecture series)
   Bibliography
   Includes index.
   1. Gardens,
ISBN 0-8076-0931-5
ISBN 0-8076-0933-pbk.

Front cover subject: *Bahran Gur Visits the Persian Princess in the Purple Palace.* Courtesy of The Metropolitan Museum of Art.
Back cover subject: Waterchutes from main platform of the Babur gardens at Dholpur. Photo: Elizabeth B. Moynihan
Frontispiece subject: Detail from the margin, leaf from the *Album of Jahangir, ca.* 1600. Courtesy of the Nelson Gallery-Atkins Museum, Kansas City, Missouri. Nelson Fund.

Book design by Nancy Kirsh

Printed in the United States of America

First Edition

Contents

Preface

Although familiar with European gardens, and a student of their history, I was unfamiliar with the Paradise Garden before our family moved to India early in 1973. At the time, I was a member of the Landscape Design Seminar at the Radcliffe Institute. As a possible independent study project for the Institute program in landscape architecture, I undertook a study of surviving Mughal gardens in India.

These geometrically laid out, enclosed water gardens are so foreign to the Indian environment that they are almost startling. As my fascination with them increased I sought out ruins as well. Intrigued by the symbolic nature of the gardens, I attempted to trace their origins by working backwards from the seventeenth century through Central Asia and Persia to ancient Mesopotamia and the concept of Paradise as a Garden—one of mankind's oldest ideals.

Through this long period, four men had a special association with the tradition of the Paradise Garden: Cyrus the Great, founder of the Persian Empire; Timur (Tamerlane) of Central Asia; Babur, the first Mughal ruler in India; and Shah Abbas who transformed Isfahan into a garden city in the seventeenth century. The first three rulers were courageous, clever and charismatic; they left their province, founded new empires, and introduced the Paradise Garden tradition to other parts of the world.

The most splendid old Paradise gardens are those of Mughal India. In India in 1974, however, there were no authentic remains of a garden built by Babur, although he described building several gardens in his autobiography, the *Babur-Nama*. After reviewing the available literature, I felt there could exist a site where his design might be preserved, thus providing an important link between the Paradise gardens of Persia and Samarkand and those of Mughal India.

In 1978, I visited Samarkand and other cities in what is now Uzbekistan, Soviet Central Asia, the area of Transoxiana where Babur was born and raised. I then returned to Kabul where he had ruled, and traveled by land to India which he conquered. The old routes used in the sixteenth century sometimes cross restricted areas, so it is not possible to trace Babur's route exactly, although some halting places and garden sites can be identified. Using a map made from the *Babur-Nama*, I followed the trail to the site of Babur's Lotus Garden at Dholpur which had been forgotten for centuries and was presumed to have disappeared entirely. There, I found several rock-cut elements, just as Babur described them!

Such a journey would have been impossible without the splendid translation of the *Babur-Nama* completed by Annette S. Beveridge in 1921. Babur's auto-biography, written in his native Turki, was translated into Persian for his grandson, the Emperor Akbar; illustrated copies from that era have survived. In the nineteenth century, the *Babur-Nama* and several other manuscripts of the sixteenth and seventeenth century were translated by scholars working for the British Crown in India. The original manuscripts are detailed, the language is occasionally confusing and frequently obscure, and some seemingly unimportant observations—including references to gardens—often do not appear in the translations (perhaps because the government was more concerned with details of tax-collecting and the military). In her translation, Mrs. Beveridge not only succeeded in preserving valuable details about gardens but captured the full range of Babur's extraordinary personality.

This book is not intended as a guide, but rather as an attempt to trace the development of the Paradise Garden. A truly remarkable aspect of these gardens is their uniformity of design throughout the centuries and across so large an area of the world with so unsettled a history. That very consistency presents a problem in writing about them, as Victoria Sackville-West has pointed out: "There is very little else to be said for the Persian garden, except to say the same thing over and over again."

Mindful of this comment, I have chosen not to describe every garden here; instead, I have included a detailed description of each type—a palace garden, a tomb garden and a pleasure garden. However, unusual features of other gardens are discussed.

One further difficulty that should be noted was the inconsistency in the spelling of words transliterated from the Persian. In a direct quote, the original spelling has been used; otherwise, the spelling is that which is in general use in each country.

The study of gardens is a field which has traditionally welcomed the amateur, and I am grateful for this openness. I should like to thank those professionals who have been so generous, especially Professor David Bates, Director of the L. H. Bailey Hortorium, Cornell University, for his comments on the native ranges of some trees and plants.

Professors Gerald Brown, Richard N. Frye, Diana Eck, and Dr. Esin Atil kindly provided help with ancient languages and obscure words. It was not only instructive but a joy to examine illustrated manuscripts, and for this I thank Robert Skelton and Betty Tyres of the Victoria and Albert Museum and Norah Titley of the British Museum.

For assistance in viewing other material and paintings, I would like to thank Mildred Archer of the India Office Library, Ralph Pinder-Wilson, Director of the British Institute of Afghan Studies, Mme. Busson of the Musée Guimet, Mme. Bernus-Taylor of the Musée du Louvre, Dr. V. Agarwal, Director of the State

Museums in Rajasthan, and the staff of the National Museum in New Delhi. I am also grateful to the library staff of the Archaeological Survey of India, and I found the Library of Congress an invaluable resource.

In Iran, Professor M. Brambilla was generous with advice, and I should like to thank Mr. B. Shirazi and his colleagues, all of whom are working on restoration, for being so helpful. Mr. A. Ebrahami and Mr. I. Amiri were informative about old water systems. Mrs. S. Niamir was enthusiastic and extraordinarily generous with her time, and I am deeply appreciative of her help in arranging visits to sites.

I am especially grateful to Dr. Galina Pugachenkova for giving me not only her time but for making material available in Uzbekistan, including the maps of Dr. M. E. Masson.

For their interest in the research on this subject of deep mutual interest, I am grateful to Dr. Javred, M. Siddique, Dr. Saifur Rahman Dar, and the late Wolf Ladejinsky. Professor Elisabeth MacDougall has been not only interested, but most encouraging.

Travel arrangements for field trips were necessarily complicated, and without the assistance of Om Prakash Gupta, Bimla Nanda Bissell, Patricia Eliot, Bruce Ehrman and John Cool, I could not have conducted the field work. I hope Harmit Singh felt rewarded for his patience and help on the frustrating last lap by the exciting moment of discovery of the Lotus Garden at Dholpur. This discovery was made possible by Hari Singh Rajoria's memory of what proved to be Babur's square well, and I should like to thank his son Najrindra for guiding us to it.

The villagers of Jhor were welcoming and generous in allowing us to investigate the site and were helpful in the initial excavations of the water chutes and pools.

I am especially thankful for comments and counsel from the readers of the manuscript: Professors Naomi Miller, J. H. Plumb, Cyrus Jhabvala, Dr. Charles Blitzer, and Maura Moynihan.

James Warren and Karen Smith were indispensable in their help with illustrations and the manuscript, and Bill Morvek of Image performed a miracle in producing photographs almost lost by a faulty light meter. Without Midge Decter's initial prodding and Jane Otten's constant encouragement, this book would not have been written. My editor, Elizabeth Hock, is not only highly professional but has been enthusiastic throughout.

My husband has been encouraging, interested and patient, and has unhesitatingly supported my research. I am, most of all, grateful to him for taking me to India.

To my companions in the search for lost gardens, I should like to dedicate this book.

Elizabeth B. Moynihan
Pindar's Corners,
New York

Introduction

I. The Sources

The English word "paradise" is simply a transliteration of the Old Persian word *pairidaeza* referring to a walled garden. It comes to us through Xenophon, the Greek essayist and historian, who heard it in 401 B.C. in Persia where he fought with Greek mercenaries. In Xenophon's Socratic Discourse, the *Oeconomicus*, Socrates explains that the Persian king not only excelled in the art of war but in cultivation, and regarded it as a noble and necessary pursuit: "In whatever countries the king resides, or wherever he travels, he is concerned that there be gardens, the so-called pleasure gardens, filled with all the fine and good things that the earth wishes to bring forth, and in these he himself spends most of his time, when the season of the year doesn't preclude it."[1] In this passage, Xenophon used the word παραδεισος for garden, or to use the Roman alphabet, *paradeisoi*.

Socrates follows this statement with an illustration by repeating a story told by the Spartan, Lysander, commander of the Peloponnesian Fleet and victor in the War. In 407 B.C., Lysander visited the Persian, Cyrus the Younger, at his palace in Sardis. When the bejeweled and elegant Cyrus showed him his pleasure garden, "Lysander had wondered at it—that the trees should be so fine, the plantings so regular, the rows of trees so straight, the angles so finely laid, and that so many pleasant scents should accompany them as they walked—wondering at these things, he spoke, 'I, Cyrus, am full of wonder at the beauty of everything, but much more do I admire the one who has measured out and ordered each kind of thing for you.' On hearing this, Cyrus was pleased and spoke. 'All these things, Lysander, I measured out and ordered myself, and there are some of them,' he said, that 'I even planted myself.'"

Cyrus called his garden a pairidaeza, which is a simple combination of pairi (around) and daeza (wall). From the Greek paradeisoi, this became the Latin paradisus, and first appeared in Middle English as paradis in 1175 in a Biblical passage: "God ha hine brohte into paradis."[2]

Some years after his Persian expedition when he settled on his estate in Scillus, Xenophon laid out a garden. He included a pairidaeza similar to Cyrus' by planting a grove of symmetrically arranged fruit trees surrounding a temple dedicated to Artemis. Xenophon's description of Cyrus' pairidaeza, as well as the beauty of his own garden, influenced the design of Greek gardens and the later gardens of Rome. Xenophon's writings were popular with the Romans, and it is believed they inspired Virgil to plant a *paradisus* of a similar grove about a Roman temple. Thus, the word "paradise" came into Western languages meaning an enclosed Persian-style garden with groves of trees.

The oldest Persian garden for which it is possible to make a schematic reconstruction was built by Cyrus the Great at Pasargadae more than 2,500 years ago, around 546 B.C. Designed to complement buildings, Cyrus' garden actually united the official and residential palaces. The geometric plan of the garden was defined by a decorative, carved stone watercourse; trees and shrubs were planted symmetrically in plots. These were the essential elements in the design of subsequent Persian gardens, which inspired the gardens of the Islamic world, most notably the great gardens of Mughal India.

A mystical feeling for flowers and a love of gardens are ancient Persian characteristics. The design of the garden, developed early and perfected to satisfy Persian taste and needs, persisted. In this as in many other artistic traditions, the Persians were conventional: when a design was perfected, it was seldom changed. The Persians were restricted by a harsh climate as well as a conservative tradition, and apparently their gardens were not horticulturally innovative.[3]

The form of the Paradise Garden evolved from the traditions of the early desert dwellers of the Near East. From earliest times, religious symbolism had exerted a powerful influence on their design. In Antiquity there existed a pantheon of gods; frequently there were many symbols for each. It is beyond the scope of this book to trace, examine or even attempt to list all of the related symbols. We are only concerned here with those which relate to objects or traditions incorporated into the gardens.[4]

The reverence for water, the mystical feeling for trees, the symbolic division of the earth into quarters by the four rivers of life and the significance of a mountain are among the most ancient and enduring traditions of the Near East, but to us the most important is yet another—the Paradise myth, the vision of Paradise as a garden. Herein lies the essential point which this volume will try to elucidate.

II. The Paradise Myth

The idea of Paradise as a garden is one of man's oldest ideals. Since the beginning of history, most probably in prehistory, societies which had nothing else in common shared the concept of Paradise as the ideal garden, a secure and everlasting garden. Almost universal in human experience, this concept of Paradise in which man transcends his frail human condition, has persisted while many of the civilizations which adhered to it have disappeared. Belief in the myth has lessened the pain of life and fear of death. The image of a place of perfect and eternal peace and plenty can make a difficult temporal existence meaningful and its transitory nature acceptable.

Ivory plate. Assur, ca. 1243–1207 B.C. Mountain with water god, flanked by trees and decorated with sun symbol. Flowing vases symbolize the four rivers of life. (Staatliche Museum, Berlin)

The Paradise myth appears in the first known writing of mankind, the wedge-shaped impressions of Mesopotamia from the proto-literate period of Sumer. Among the oldest Sumerian cuneiform tablets unearthed and deciphered is a 278-line poem of the Sumerian paradise myth: Dilmun was a land that was "pure, clear and bright," whose fortunate inhabitants knew neither sickness, violence nor aging, but which had no fresh water. The Sumerian God of Water, Enki, ordered the Sun God, Utu, to create a divine garden by providing fresh water from beneath the earth; Utu obeyed and Dilmun was transformed into a Paradise of the Gods with fruit trees, green fields, and meadows.[5]

In the twenty-seventh century B.C., the dominant Sumerian city state of Erech (Warka, Iraq) was ruled by Gilgamesh. Gilgamesh later became the hero of the collected myths of the Akkadians and Babylonians. Many of these myths develop the theme of death and immortality and the hope of eternal return. The Paradise myth is repeated on fragments of Babylonian tablets bearing the *Epic of Gilgamesh*. In the following excerpt, Gilgamesh wanders in the Garden of the Gods:

> And lo! the gesdin [tree] shining stands
> With crystal branches in the golden sands,
> In this immortal garden stands the Tree,
> With trunk of gold, and beautiful to see.
> Beside a sacred fount the tree is placed,
> With emeralds and unknown gems is graced.[6]

Seal impression. Late Akkadian, *ca.* 2254–2154 B.C. Heroes with symbols of the water god. Note vase with flowing water. (Courtesy of the Metropolitan Museum of Art, Lent by the Right Reverend Paul Moore, Jr., 1955)

The Sumerian-Babylonian Paradise, the Garden of the Gods, was an idyllic earthly garden of peace and plenty reserved for those who had achieved immortality. It corresponds to the Homeric Elysian Fields—a place of perfect bliss and immortality for those favored by the gods.[7] This ancient mythological theme—the promise of Paradise as a garden—is surely one of the most beautiful that man has ever created. For primitive people living the hard life of the soil— people who feared the natural world and dreaded the unknown—it was a green and hopeful myth.

The colorful, dramatic *Epic* was popular and widely known throughout the ancient world and influenced the folk-tales of later civilizations. Under the Achaemenid kings of Persia (sixth to fourth centuries B.C.) the prophet Zarathustra, known to us by the Greek name, Zoroaster, gained prominence. The *Avesta*, the later collected holy works of the Zoroastrians, records a promise by the prophet of a paradise with paths of burnished gold, pleasure pavilions of diamonds and filled with fruit and fragrant flowers. The Yashts, or heroic hymns of the *Avesta*, parallel the hymns of the *Rig-Veda* of ancient India. Both contain heroic exploits similar to the *Epic of Gilgamesh*, as do the legends of the Greeks, especially those relating the labors of Heracles.

The *Epic* was certainly familiar to the Jews during their Babylonian captivity, from which the first Achaemenid king, Cyrus the Great, released them in 538 B.C. and allowed them to return to Jerusalem. In the Old Testament, the Hebrew word *pardes*, from the Old Persian pairidaeza, is used to mean garden. It was in the Greek translation of the Old Testament—with its use of the word *paradeisos* for garden—that Paradise became identified with the Garden of Eden, where

4

primeval man dwelt in the gardens of the Lord. Through the Bible, earthly Paradise became identified with Heaven—the celestial abode of God—remote and unobtainable, thus acquiring the transcendental image dominant in Christian tradition.

Mircea Eliade has written that the "Nostalgia for Paradise" is one of the oldest types of Christian mystical experience. He defines this nostalgia as "man's repeated attempt to re-establish the paradisal situation lost at the dawn of time," and believes it existed almost everywhere in primitive societies.[8] Eliade reaffirms the prevalence of this belief in "The Myth of Eternal Return." Such return is found in Indian philosophy where the end of one cycle is the beginning of the next. In the Paradise myth, the Garden of Paradise—the primeval beginning—is the final reward.

The sacred vision of the Garden of Paradise varied from a single place of total bliss to several gardens of varying degrees of bliss. In the New Testament, Paul refers to a man caught up in the "third heaven" of Paradise.[9] The Paradise promised in the Koran consists of several terraces of gardens, each more splendid than the last. In the Islamic gardens in Persia and Mughal India, the terraces were often meant to correspond to the enclosures which made up the Garden of Paradise in the Koran.[10]

III. Water and Trees

Water was ever dominant, the central and most essential element in the Persian garden. Indeed, since the first settlements were established in the Near East, water had been the controlling force in the lives of the people.

In the earliest known civilization of lower Mesopotamia the "land between the rivers"—the Tigris and the Euphrates—people believed that water was the source of all life, an idea common in many ancient cultures. For the Mesopotamian people, water—through irrigation—made cultivation of the great alluvial river basin possible. Early communities were evidently democratic: every man cooperated to build and maintain the canals, dykes, and reservoirs or earthen tanks, on which crops and life depended. Violent floods occurred periodically and were disastrous. Thus, through dependence and fear, these primitive cultivators developed a reverence for water. One of their earliest deities was the god of sweet water, whom they also regarded as the friend and protector of man.

Nature myths, which endured for centuries, were among the early oral traditions in this archaic Mesopotamian civilization. Plants and trees not only symbolized vegetation deities, but were believed to contain a divine presence.

Early Sumerian tablets often illustrate the exalted position of the tree. On one such tablet the mystical Huluppu tree is uprooted by the south wind and carried by the waters of the Euphrates until the goddess of love and fertility "seized the tree in her hand and brought it to Uruk: 'To pure Inanna's holy garden thou shalt bring it.' "[11]

As religious ritual developed, votive trees gained prominence, and led to the worship of the cosmologically sacred tree. The miraculous Cosmic Tree, a common mythical motif found throughout the world, has survived to the present day. Usually it represents regeneration or immortality, but it has also been found

Stone fountain. Mari, *ca.* 2125–2025 B.C. Water was piped through a hole in the base and flowed from the vase held by the goddess. The flowing vase as the symbol of the source of all water, therefore the source of life, appears consistently in the art of West Asia. (Aleppo Museum)

to symbolize the heavens or a means of ascent to heaven. Occasionally, as in the ancient Brahmanical tradition of India or the Shamanism of Central Asia, the sacred tree was considered the symbolic axis of the world.

Sacred trees are mentioned in the sacred literature of the world's major religions, as the Tree of Knowledge, or the Tree of Good and Evil. In Revelation (22:1—2) the tree of life is associated with the river of life. The Koran (13:28) mentions the Tuba tree in Paradise. The Cosmic Tree has appeared as an inverted tree with its roots in heaven, growing downward toward the earth as depicted in the Upanishads of ancient India and in medieval Kabbalistic writings.

If archaeologists are the detectives who trace man's past, then pottery fragments are the clues by which bygone cultures are interpreted. Fragments of fine pottery decorated with cosmological trees have been found at archaeological sites of settlements dating from the third and fourth millennia. Dr. Phyllis Ackerman studied the astral significance of trees in the iconography of this pottery and developed an enchanting explanation of the "Tree of Life" or "Moon Tree." She concluded that the early Mesopotamian settlers conceived of the sky

"Tree Worship," Bikaner 1700. The festival of Amla Ekadasi, when women present offerings to the Amla tree. (Collection of Paul Walter)

as a triangle and depicted it as a mountain. The moon, which brought relief from the relentless sun, was depicted as a tree atop the mountain of the sky. As trees mark an oasis and the moon is a life-giver, so the sap of the moon tree must be water—the elixir of life.[12]

Thus, the symbolic relationship of trees and water was well established over five thousand years ago. Use of a familiar object to symbolize the distant and mysterious moon enabled early man not only to comprehend his world but to feel more secure in it. The bull and the ibex were widely used animal symbols for the moon; the volute of their horns represents the moon's crescents. It appears that the cyclic pattern of the moon was realized quite early; people linked its rhythm to the cycles of women and plants, and its waning to death.

Since prehistoric times there has been communication and mutual cultural influence among the civilizations of the Indus Valley and those of Mesopotamia and the Iranian plateau. Archeologists found evidence confirming trade among them when they discovered Indus Valley seals of the third millennium at Susa I (modern Sush). These seals were incised with a Moon Tree resembling the peepul tree native to the subcontinent. In Persia, the Moon Tree was drawn as a conifer— possibly a cypress—which came to symbolize immortality in Persian culture. Cypress trees inevitably appear in Persian and Mughal gardens; great avenues of cypress often border the watercourses which divide the garden into plots. Thus the association of the tree of immortality with water, the elixir of life, continued.

Drawings from seal impressions found at Susa. *Ca.* early third millennium B.C.
    a. Indus valley seal with peepul tree represented by a leaf growing into the ground.
    b. Persian seal with cypress tree on top of a mountain, flanked by ibex.

IV. The Mountain of Paradise and The Four Rivers of Life

In Book IV of *Paradise Lost*, Milton described a vision of Paradise as having the "goodliest Trees loaden with fairest Fruit." In 1667, then, the idea was still intact, still as vital as it had been in Sumer almost 4,500 years earlier.

Within "delicious Paradise," Milton envisioned:

Southward through Eden went a River large,
Nor chang'd his course, but through the shaggie hill
Pass'd underneath ingulft, for God had thrown
That Mountain as his Garden mould high rais'd
Upon the rapid current, which through veins
Of porous Earth with kindly thirst up drawn,
Rose a fresh Fountain, and with many a rill
Water'd the Garden; thence united fell
Down the steep glade, and met the nether Flood,
Which from his darksom passage now appeers,
And now divided into four main Streams.

This vision of Paradise illustrates two other ancient images: The Mountain of Paradise and the Four Rivers of Life.[13]

The idea of the sacred mount is common and is represented in the sacred architecture of many cultures. Scholars have interpreted the Mesopotamian *ziggurats*, or staged temple towers, as representing mountains. For the Babylonians, the ziggurat was the bond between the vault of the heavens and the earth.

Sanchi. First half of the second century B.C. The function of the funerary stupa, which represents the fixed cosmic structure, was to guard a relic. Its precise proportions were fixed in elaborate, geometric ceremonies.

The Buddhist *stupa*, or sacred mound, is another example. At the Dome of the Rock in Jerusalem, the mountain itself has been represented as being the center of the earth.

The Mountain of Paradise is often shown atop the rising or crossing of the four rivers which nourish life and divide the earth. The earliest expression of the idea of the four rivers dividing the earth is found on prehistoric pottery discovered beneath the ruins of the city of Samarra. These artifacts are among the most ancient in existence. One bowl bears a simple yet striking design: the crossing of two canals with trees and birds in the four corners. Professor Ernst Herzfeld has interpreted the design to be the four rivers of life—the *chahar-su*. The four rivers appear in the Vedas of ancient India and in Genesis (2:10—14). In *The City of God*, St. Augustine used the earthly Garden of Paradise as a metaphor for the Church with the four rivers symbolizing the four gospels.

A division of the earth into quarters was first associated with kingship around 2500 B.C. when the Akkadian kings began proclaiming themselves "King of the Four Quarters." Another version of such division can be found in Hindu tradition with four divine abodes, *char dham*, one at each compass point. In the Paradise Garden, the crossing of the watercourses represents the four rivers of life.

V. The Gardens

In the historic lands once peopled by the ancient Mesopotamians, the great rivers have shifted, the delta has changed, and the desert has spread. Once there may have been tracts of trees and wide grazing lands, but the rains were only seasonal, and the sun baked the earth for the greater part of the year. It was always a harsh climate and a dry land, and man learned early to wall out the hostile world of sandy winds and predators, animal and human. Sticks, reeds, and the mud brick were his building materials. Ruins of settlements of the sixth millennium have been uncovered and found to have had massive defensive mud walls. Excavations of primitive settlements in Mesopotamia and Central Asia have unearthed houses with walled enclosures or courts almost identical to village houses found throughout the Near East today. Within the security of their walls, their supply of water assured, the people were free to worship the symbol of their gods, sometimes a water goddess, sometimes the sacred tree.

The wild grasses first tamed by man were the ancestors of wheat and barley and were native to the Near East.[14] Successful farming by irrigation caused the area to prosper; hence the population increased, leading city-states to war with each other for new territory. Thus the agricultural life of the early settlements was disrupted as kingship and the warlike skills of the people developed; successive warrior kings were overthrown by others equally rapacious. Trade and domestic skills, however, managed to advance.

In tenth-century B.C. Babylon, 10,000 square miles of land were under cultivation through irrigation. The French archaeologist G. Contenau deciphered a tablet which relates the passionate interest in botany of a Babylonian king who maintained and even catalogued a garden of culinary and medicinal specimen plants. Sennacherib (706–681 B.C.) built an aqueduct in Nineveh to carry water to his groves of date palms.[15]

The inhabitants of the Iranian plateau were agriculturalists as early as the fourth millennium. Excavations at Siyalk, southeast of Tehran, revealed a crude settlement with stone sickle blades dating from the end of the neolithic age. In the fourth millennium, the plough had replaced the digging stick, and cast and socketed metal hoes were used.[16]

It was not until the beginning of the first millennium that the Aryans migrated to the lands between the Ganges and the Euphrates. The nomadic Aryans were absorbed into the existing communities on the Iranian plateau and adopted the settled life and many traditions of the agricultural people they conquered.

Theologians disagree about the exact nature of their religion but generally concur that the Aryan gods were identified with nature. Moreover, it is believed that the Aryans dominated the civilization which developed on the plateau to the extent that their Indo-European dialect became the language. In this new civilization, gardens assumed great importance.[17]

On the plateau, the southwestern province of Parsa (modern Fars) was the home of the Aryan Achaemenians; it was known to the Greeks as Persis. After 546 B.C., when Cyrus the Great conquered the neighboring realms and established the Achaemenid Empire, the province gave its name to the entire country—

Seal impression. Achaemenid *ca.* 540–450 B.C. Achaemenid king slaying a Greek warrior. Note tree. The palm as represented here consistently recurs in West Asian art, often associated with royalty. (Courtesy of The Metropolitan Museum of Art, Lent by the Right Reverend Paul Moore, Jr., 1955)

Persia. Persian history and the history of Persian gardens begin with the Achaemenians, the greatest gardeners of the ancient world.

It is my purpose here to show the continuity of the tradition and symbolic topography of the Paradise Garden. Such continuity is understandable because the Paradise Garden is derived from native conventions; they were not merely for royal enjoyment. Other gardens have existed in developing societies throughout history, but they were enjoyed by royalty and the nobility and were usually built only in times of peace. In Persia the tradition of gardens was not exclusively aristocratic; gardens were found connected to simple homes as well. Arthur Upham Pope has written: "Indeed, in domestic architecture, change has been slight throughout thousands of years. The old Iranian house with its grim outer walls and its garden and court within, is the same yesterday, today and forever, and has even been so ensconced in national habit that it has controlled the ground-plan of various kinds of public buildings, like the great Islamic *madrasas* and *caravanserais*." [18]

Persian culture is unique in its strength and resilience; its influence often extended beyond the Iranian plateau even when its political influence did not. This culture has, of course, been enriched by that of conquered nations, as well as by conquerors. Though Persia suffered centuries of war and domination by foreign rulers, the Paradise Garden survived and was adopted by successive invaders, hence the tradition became diffused throughout the world. [19]

Though most admired for their outstanding gift for decoration, the Persians developed an architecture distinct in its monumentality and ornamentation. The enclosed Persian garden is part of this architectural heritage and became the prototype for the Islamic garden and the gardens of Mughal India. When adopted by the nature-loving nomadic Central Asians, the gardens became royal encampments. The Mughals of India, descended from the Central Asians, were the world's most elegant nomads and used the gardens as palaces.

The ideal, the model for these gardens—the blissful Paradise, a garden of perpetual spring—was the reward in the afterlife. Paradoxically, the earthly, verdant Paradise Garden which affirmed a love of nature, was a celebration of life. With their symbolic trees reaching toward the heavens, the purling water and fragrant flowers, these gardens never acquired an entirely secular character. This explains why the fundamental geometric design has not changed.

The oldest surviving garden tradition, the Paradise Garden is still influential and flourishing today.

PERSIA

ONE

The Achaemenians: Empire

The Iranian plateau is not an auspicious place for a garden. There is very little rainfall—two to ten inches annually during the cold winter months. The annual change in temperature is severe: bitter winters are followed by dry summers and scorching sun. Throughout the year harsh winds buffet the plateau. These conditions make it particularly difficult to cultivate a garden. It is not hard to understand, therefore, why the Persians have always loved their gardens and flowers so passionately.

The center of the Iranian plateau averages between four and five thousand feet in elevation and is an elongated saucer of salt and gravel desert basins with folded hills. It is almost completely ringed by mountains which shield it from rain-bearing winds. From the Persian Gulf in the south, the wide parallel ranges of the Zagros mountains form the barrier to the arid central land. In the north, the steep Elbruz chain separates the central desert from a narrow strip of lush vegetation along the Caspian Coast. The Elbruz ends in sight of the Hindu Kush to the east. The violent winds in the northeast uplands render them nearly uninhabitable. There are few rivers in Iran; the isolated fertile valleys in the mountains are watered by snows. Cultivation depends almost entirely on irrigation though there are some areas which are suitable for grazing part of the year, and these have always supported a nomadic population. The non-nomadic communities are located at the base of the mountain chains fringing the central deserts. The most remarkable feature of the plateau is not its geography but its light; for thousands of years it has astonished travelers by its brilliance.

While its ancient history continues to be unravelled, we know that Persia's emergence as an empire in the sixth century B.C. began on the plain of Murghab, the scene of Cyrus the Great's victory over the Medes in 550 B.C.

Cyrus was hardly more than a boy when he defeated the ruling Medes and conquered Lydia. Then in an astonishingly brief period—less than ten years—he subdued the tribes of eastern Iran and conquered the Babylonians, ending forever the Mesopotamian dominance in the world. A political, as well as a military genius, Cyrus successfully united this vast territory into the first world empire. An

Pasargadae. Standing column
of palace.

unvengeful victor, he spared the lives and cities of defeated kings and treated
them with respect. He built his capital *ca.* 546 B.C. in his native province of Fars
and gave it the name of his tribe, *Pasargadae.*

The site of Pasargadae is peaceful yet majestic, situated as it is at the foot of
mountains which encircle—rather than enclose—the fertile, gently-rolling plain.
Archaeological investigations have established that the plain, which is watered by
the Pulvar River, was farmed before the third millennium B.C. Birds wheel and
swoop along the banks of the Pulvar; only their cries break the stillness.

One gleaming white column soars above the stone platform of Cyrus the
Great's ruined palace. Starkly dramatic against the enameled azure sky, it is
topped by the untidy nest of a stork—the sole guardian of all that is left of Cyrus'
capital. Historically, Persians regarded storks as good omens; although at first the
great bird's bulky nest seems incongruous, it is somehow fitting in this pastoral
setting of the first capital of the Achaemenids.

Gardens are the most impermanent of man's architectural creations. It is
therefore remarkable that the outline of so much of Cyrus' 2,500-year-old royal
garden may still be seen today. Several long sections of the limestone waterways
remain, their course interrupted almost every fifty feet by basins about one meter
square, each cut from a single stone block. The broken lines of bright, white

15

Pasargadae. Water basin and remains of stone watercourse.

stone stand out against the dark green scrubby growth between the platforms of the ruined pavilions and palaces.

"The palaces of Cyrus were designed as open, crystalline structures with a new, four-sided character." So writes Dr. David Stronach of the British Institute of Persian Studies. He continues, "Such buildings invited inspection from every direction, and in keeping with the generous proportions of the site, care was taken to place them in spacious, well-watered grounds. Indeed, the available evidence suggests that each inner palace with its stately colonnades and deep, shadowed porticos was first glimpsed amidst a profusion of trees, shrubs and grasses."[1]

The architectural remains of the innovative black and white limestone palaces gleam in the radiant light of the plateau. Their close relationship with the gardens is clear, as can be seen on the site plan. Even more important in the garden scheme were the two pavilions. The rectangular platforms of dressed stones which remain indicate that each of the buildings had columned porticoes and consisted of one room with thick walls of mud brick; wide opposing doorways led off the longer porticoes. This design remained the model for garden pavilions for centuries.

The design of the royal complex is unified by the watercourse. Dr. Stronach found that the known watercourse of the garden covered a length of over 1,100 meters. The construction was simple: the stone blocks were laid directly on the earth with only a small number of basins set on a layer of supporting stones. The original drainage slope of the gravity-fed water system appears to have been slight, and Dr. Stronach suggests that the deep basins may have helped keep the shallow channels free of silt.

The hydraulic system at Pasargadae was carefully planned. It was not a functional need for irrigation which dictated the geometric pattern of the layout; open ditches irrigated the plantings. The stone waterchannels served a purely decorative purpose. Though our knowledge of details of Persian gardens built

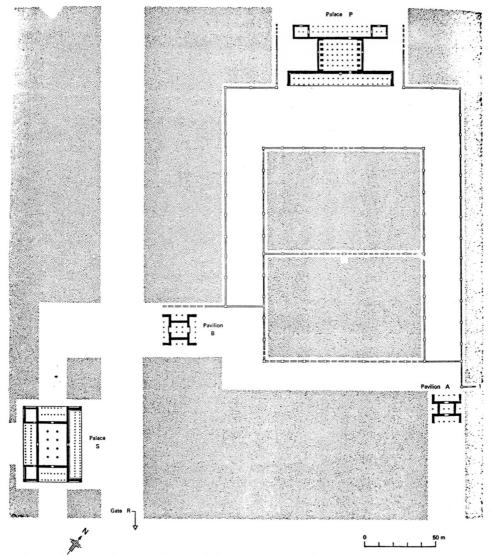

Pasargadae. Sketch plan of the Royal Garden. The lines of the paths are conjectural.

during the next 1,700 years is sketchy, we do know that the style of the water-channels changed very little. As in this royal garden at Pasargadae, the watercourse continued to define the geometric plan of the garden.

We can only speculate how Cyrus used this garden, but there is evidence to suggest that it was meant to be viewed from the airy buildings rather than enjoyed as a place for activities. The royal residents could recline within the deeply shaded pavilions and enjoy breezes carrying the fragrance of the aromatic wild grasses and herbaceous shrubs waving beneath the rows of fruit trees.

This manner of enjoying a garden was characteristic of the generations of

17

Tehran, Iran. Modern garden.

Hasan Abal, Pakistan. Wah Bagh,
late sixteenth century.

later Persians. In an essay on Persian gardens, Victoria Sackville-West described the feeling a Persian has for his garden: "It is not a place where he wants to stroll; it is a place where he wants to sit and entertain his friends with conversation, music, philosophical discourse, and poetry; and if he can watch the spring rain pouring down, so much the better, for he knows it will not come again for months and months and months."[2]

We must also speculate on the trees and flowers planted in the royal garden. The pomegranate undoubtedly was prominent at Pasargadae. Native to Persia and the Near East, it had been cultivated for centuries. Another native tree, the sour cherry, so popular in later gardens for its rounded shape, moderate height, and clusters of white flowers, may have blossomed in Cyrus' garden. In Mesopotamia the vine had been cultivated since the third millennium; native to the plateau, it was surely included. Several native herbaceous plants of the pea family, including some clovers, could have mingled with the fragrant grasses mentioned by Arrian and other classical historians. The large lily family has many native Persian members including a tulip, an exceedingly tall lily, and a ground-hugging lily. Several irises are among the many other flowers native to Iran as is the common, fragrant, white jasmine.

But which rose blossomed in the emperor's garden? Given the special fondness of Persians for the rose, it must have been prominent, though we do not know in what form. Perhaps the lovely, single, yellow rose which still grows wild in Iran.

Some small distance from the palaces at Pasargadae stands Cyrus' tomb. In the spring of 330 B.C., another conqueror and king, Alexander of Macedon, was pursuing the vanquished Darius III, the last Achaemenian, and paused at Pasargadae to pay homage at the tomb of Cyrus. "The tomb of this Cyrus was in the territory of the Pasargadae, in the royal park; round it had been planted a grove of all sorts of trees; the grove was irrigated, and deep grass had grown in the meadow; the tomb itself was built, at the base, with stones cut square and raised into rectangular form."[3] The tomb and the surrounding grove were set within an enclosure as was a small building set aside for the Magians, or priests who were the hereditary guardians of the tomb.

Alexander was distressed to find the tomb of Cyrus broken into and rifled. The tomb itself was a small chamber on a high-stepped stone plinth "with a door leading into it so narrow that with difficulty, and after great trouble, one man, and he a small one, could enter. And in the chamber was placed a golden sarcophagus, in which Cyrus' body had been buried."[4]

Aristobulus recorded that on instructions from Alexander he passed through this entrance and restored the tomb. He saw the following inscription carved in Persian on the tomb: "O man, I am Cyrus who acquired the empire for the Persians and was king of Asia; grudge me not, therefore, my monument."[5]

Plutarch wrote that "The reading of this sensibly touched Alexander, filling him with the thought of the uncertainty and mutability of human affairs."[6]

Cyrus' tomb became a pilgrimage site for the later Achaemenids; Darius I and Cyrus III made frequent visits here. In the sanctuary of the nearby temple dedicated to the goddess Anahita, his successors were invested with Cyrus' robe; during the ritual the new king ate a cake of figs, chewed turpentine wood, and drank a cup of sour milk. From these early times, groves of trees in symmetrical arrangement appear to have provided a setting considered suitable for rituals.

The description of the Pairidaeza at Pasargadae is similar to that given by Xenophon of Cyrus III's Pairidaeza at Sardis which emphasized the symmetrical planting of trees in rows and the use of herbaceous shrubs. This is an indication of a continuity in the treatment of plant material by the Achaemenids.

Though his life of Cyrus, the *Cyropaedia*, written after 394 B.C., is fictional, Xenophon drew on his travels in the Achaemenid Empire for descriptions of Persia. His references to the parks of the Persian kings and accounts of later classical writers mention animals grazing among the trees, and tell us the enclosures were large enough for the king to enjoy a chase. In the *Cyropaedia*, Xenophon mentions such a park of Astyges, the Median king who was Cyrus' grandfather.[7] Such references to the gardens of the Medes are particularly important for they are all we have, there being neither ruins nor Persian descriptions.

It is not certain whether a symmetrical grove of trees, as that which surrounded Cyrus' tomb, was of an older Median tradition that he adopted, or whether it was an innovation of his descendants. We know that it was well established by 401 B.C. when Xenophon first saw it.

The wall carvings of the early Persians were ceremonial. And as they left no descriptive wall paintings, commentaries or journals, we must look to the classical writers and examine ruins to recreate the design and character of early gardens.[8] In so doing, we find constant affirmation of the mystical importance of gardens to the Persians. As Arthur Upham Pope has written, "The fertility theme continued to be central in the life of the plateau peoples, and the artistic forms which they invented to envisage these principles, sanctified by long use and deep emotion, provided figures and motifs that persisted throughout the entire course of Iranian art. All the rich representations of floral abundance, the various cosmological trees, the exaltation of the garden, the poetic flower worship, which has dominated both decorative and representative arts almost to the present day, were but phases of the appeal for sustenance."[9]

The mystical appeal of the garden is manifested in its close relationship with adjacent buildings. This relationship is evident in the schematic reconstruction of Pasargadae and in ruins dating from the centuries following the Achaemenid reign to the present day. The relationship of garden, buildings, and watercourse remained the essential feature of the archetypal royal garden.

Differing from the large gardens such as Pasargadae, which surrounded the buildings, small gardens enclosed within the palace were built. These small gardens were similar to the domestic gardens built by ordinary citizens. As in the royal complex, a close relationship has always existed between the building and the garden in domestic Persian architecture. Traditionally, Persian houses were positioned at the end of a garden and had a raised, recessed platform, called a *talar*, overlooking a pool or watercourse in the garden. Shade trees bordered the symmetrically laid out paths in the garden and the high mud walls; fruit trees were planted in the plots. Varieties of flowers were mixed and naturalized beneath the trees—that is, scattered to resemble natural growth. The talar and its adjacent garden could be used as an extension of the house, indeed another room, for much of the year. The recessed talars of larger houses often had columns and, therefore, resembled in design the porticoes of royal pavilions. Both served the same purpose: they provided a raised, shaded view of the garden.

One such small garden, with sections of a carved stone waterchannel and basins, was found in Darius I's private quarters in the palace of his capital at Persepolis. Not enclosed in the building, however, it was adjacent to the king's apartment and enclosed by a wall. A network of huge underground conduits, fed by cisterns, carried water through the broad stone platform to the baths, palaces, and gardens.

The third Achaemenid emperor, Darius I (521–485 B.C.), was a gifted statesman and administrator and among the greatest rulers of Asia. Though reputedly a follower of Zoroastrian doctrines, he allowed conquered people, such as the Egyptians and the Semitic races, to continue traditional religious practices. In a gesture characteristic of Asian kings, he built a new capital—far more elaborate than Pasargadae—some thirty miles to the southwest at Persepolis. The royal complex was constructed on a platform of monolithic stones carved out of the foothills of the mountains north of the Marv Dasht plain, the site of prehistoric settlements.

Persepolis is not human in scale; it is clearly a ceremonial capital, and it is generally believed that it was built for the observance of No Ruz, or the new year, when the arrival of spring is celebrated. Preparations for the feast are depicted in relief on the ceremonial staircases of the audience chambers. On one parapet, the officers of the king's guard are seen chatting in line and carrying flowers in procession. For this festival, representatives of subject nations brought gifts to the Persian king, and Indian Brahmins are shown among the tribute bearers.

By the fifth century B.C., the Persian genius for decoration was already well-developed. The low-relief figures are more decorative than sculptural. Rhythmic and beautiful as ornament, they somehow fail to capture the real joy and exuberance of the feast of No Ruz which celebrates rebirth and spring, the season when the desert miraculously bursts into bloom—a spectacle which each year enchants and lightens Persian hearts. The hope and renewal inspired by this brief, annual phenomenon is a pervasive theme in Persian art and poetry.

The lotus, the cypress, and the palm tree are carved repeatedly in orderly rows on the Persepolitan reliefs. The cypress, representing eternity, appears in paintings, on buildings, and in gardens in pre-Islamic and Islamic Persian art and later in that of the Mughals of India. The stylized cypress of Persepolis, derived from Mesopotamian art, is one of the most charming—it is plump and sturdy.

The Achaemenians used the lotus in all its forms—bud, flower, palmette; their kings are often shown holding the flower in cup form. It appeared most frequently

Persepolis. Ruins of palaces on raised stone platform. (Courtesy of the Oriental Institute, University of Chicago)

21

Persepolis. Lotus relief showing carver's mark.

Persepolis. Portions of a stone watercourse
and carved basin.

as a rosette with twelve solar petals. The pomegranate, called "The Tree of Many
Seeds," was an ancient sun symbol associated with the mysteries of fertility; but
Phyllis Ackerman writes that by the time of Darius I the lotus had almost replaced
the pomegranate as the common fertility symbol.[10]

No other flower has been so widely used and so variously and expressively
portrayed as the lotus. In ancient Egypt, it was associated with the Nile as the
giver of life. Venerable to the ancient Hindus, it was also closely identified with
the Buddha. As the sacred tree of life of the Assyrians, the lotus inspired the
Phoenician stele capital and thus, as other Near Eastern traditions, was introduced
into Western art. The familiar egg and dart design in Western decoration derives
from the Greek lotus bud and palmette form.

An overall lotus tree pattern decorates a section of surviving glazed brick
revetment from Darius' administrative capital of Susa. Begun about 521 B.C. in
the great river basin below the Iranian plateau to the west, it is possible to recreate
the scale of Susa's palaces from remaining lotus-shaped bases. Over seven feet
in diameter, they supported columns fifty feet tall. Similar in design, the palaces
and stairways of Susa surpassed the ceremonial capital of Persepolis in size and
grandeur. Darius' proud words on surviving foundation tablets record details of
construction by workmen and materials from all the countries of the empire.

A magnificent walled and moated city with extensive groves of trees in a large
Pairidaeza, Susa was famous in history and legend. Coveted by the Greeks, it was
the setting for Aeschylus' (525-456 B.C.) drama,[11] *The Persae*, which is based on

the Persian battle with the Greeks at Salamis. It is Sushan in the biblical story of Esther who married an Achaemenian king and dwelt here in a splendid palace. It was here, too, that Alexander held a mass marriage ceremony in the spring of 323 B.C. uniting ten thousand Greeks and Persians. Throughout the centuries, Susa was repeatedly damaged but rebuilt until the Mongol invasions in the early thirteenth century. Stripped of its tile and stone, its irrigation system destroyed and trees burnt, the city was gradually covered by the spreading desert. It lay forgotten until identified by the British archaeologist W. K. Loftus in 1854.

The example of Susa is typical of sites in the Near East. When unbaked brick is neglected, or tile sheathing falls off, mud walls sink back into the earth. As early as the fourth millennium B.C., mud bricks were used on the Iranian plateau. These were crude oval lumps fashioned by hand and sun dried. A few centuries later, the rectangular brick, shaped in a wooden mold, was developed. This brick is still used in Iran though the mud is mixed with straw or some other binding material. After several hours in the sun, and one turning, the bricks are ready for use.

In the summer, Persian emperors left Susa and the fierce heat of the desert and moved to the rebuilt Median capital of Ecbatana with its cool terraced gardens in the Zagros Mountains. At an altitude of six thousand feet, overlooking a plain of orchards and vineyards and watered by rivers from Mt. Orontes, it was one of the most beautifully situated cities in the empire. The Median princess who married Nebuchadrezzar and lived in sixth-century B.C. Babylon so longed

Susa. Huge mounds showing excavations. (Courtesy of the Oriental Institute, University of Chicago)

was ingenious and quite simple. A main shaft was sunk to the permanent subterranean water level, usually at the base of hills or mountains. Workers then dug a tunnel from where the water was needed to the source. At intervals of about fifty feet or less, shafts from the surface were dug to remove the excavated material and provide air for the laborers. These shafts were later used to maintain the qanat line. The tunnel was slightly inclined toward the source; hence the water system was propelled by gravity. Where the ground was particularly porous, the channels were lined with stone or tile. They varied in length from several hundred feet to many miles and were dug by hand with the simplest tools; the excavators' guide to a straight line, for example, was the shadow cast by a candle.

The failure of a qanat or a diminished flow of water meant the death of a village. The people simply moved on. This explains some of the clustered ruins of mud houses often seen today at some distance from the foothills.[17] The shafts of abandoned qanat lines were a hazard for caravans, which often crossed the desert by night, and the journals of early travelers describe both tragic and comic incidents. Often two or three qanat channels run parallel to each other, and the lines of regularly spaced mounds of earth surrounding the access shafts are an odd sight in the dun-colored desert.

With the new, deep mechanized wells and the tremendous increase in the use of water for industrialization and urbanization, the subterranean water level of the plateau has dropped sharply. As a result, many old qanats have run dry.

The simple, age-old Iranian system of watering tree roots in orchards, bordering gardens, or lining avenues, is by seepage from *jouies*, commonly called jubes. These are merely open channels which move water in furrows or shallow trenches between rows of trees. Still used in Iran, jubes can be seen today in Tehran.

Qanat lines running from base of mountains across desert.

Irrigation by qanats and jubes was introduced into other parts of the old Persian Empire, where a reliable water supply had previously been unknown. Ancient qanat lines have been discovered in southern Arabia and are found north of the Kara Kum desert on the old route to Samarkand, and in Afghanistan where they are called *kariz*. Jubes, called *aryks* in Central Asia and *juis* in Afghanistan, form the common method of watering trees in those areas today.

Oases of natural springs provided another source of irrigation and relief from the general barrenness of the arid plateau. In eastern Iran, some dependable oases which existed in ancient times still produce well-cultivated fields and nourish fine orchards which yield abundant fruit. The reliability of other oases has always varied with the infrequent rainfall. Villages and hamlets surround the oases and cluster at the foot of mountains whose streams are a source of life-giving water.

Oases were probably the first gardens. Today some are formalized with terraced gardens and enclosures, but informal gardens spring up under the date palms which invariably shade them. The date palm produces a crop important to the Persian desert dwellers and is regarded with an almost mystical affection by the Arabs who came in the seventh century. Of the Arabs in western Iran at the beginning of the nineteenth century, Sir John Malcolm wrote: "The inhabitants of the country over which we hunted are all Arabs. They live, like their brethren in other parts, almost entirely on camels' milk and dates. Their care appears limited to the preservation of the animal and the propagation of the tree, which yield what they account the best of this world's luxuries; and these not only furnish this lively race of men with food, but with almost all the metaphors in which their language abounds." [18]

Water running in a jube between rows of poplars outside walled garden.

TWO

The Sassanians: Glory

In the 2,500 years since Cyrus the Great, Persia, the strategic land bridge to Asia, had been subjected to repeated savage invasions from the east and west. The jealous empires of the west—Greek, Roman, and Turkish—and the barbaric nomads of Central Asia repeatedly sought to control the Iranian plateau. Though enriched by the culture of their conquerors, a distinct Persian culture survived long periods of foreign domination—testimony to its strength and resilience.

The power and presence of succeeding dynasties, native or foreign, were expressed in the character of the architectural styles they developed. Each, however, included the Persian garden as an integral part of palace design. The environmental factor was also important; flowing water was healthier than standing pools, and the enclosed garden was an effective means of alleviating the harsh desert climate. Thus this Persian architectural feature, deeply rooted in native tradition, survived.

Though Alexander's successors, the Selucids, ruled less than one hundred years after his death in 323 B.C., they brought more Iranian land under cultivation. Under their leadership, a period of intense agricultural development took place. They introduced triple rotation of crops, a new plough, and greater cultivation of the fruiting vine. Increased trade with the growing Roman Empire was accompanied by the introduction of many Asiatic plants to Europe. Professor R. Ghirshman has written that, "The defeated Orient subjugated Europe." Cotton, the lemon, the melon, sesame seed, the oriental nut, olives, dates, and figs were among the new plants which brought about "a real agrarian revolution in Italy."[1]

In the first century B.C., Roman warriors invaded Persia for power and plunder and were captivated by the gardens. Following his extended Eastern campaigns, the Roman general, Lucullus, returned to Rome and retired to the great gardens he built in the Persian style. He had an interest in philosophy, wrote a history, and collected a great library, but he was also famous for his expensive taste. His gardens were so large and costly to build that he was called "Xerxes in a toga" by Tubero the Stoic when he saw them.[2] Lucullus is credited with introducing the peach and the cherry to Europe in these gardens.

In the second and third centuries, Persia was ruled by the Parthians, who received embassies from China which led to the exchange of important plants. The small and graceful peach tree with its solitary pink blossoms was thus acquired from western China with the apricot, often favored for its delicate flowers and heart-shaped leaves. China in turn imported the native Persian vine, cucumber, onion, saffron, and jasmine and began cultivation of alfalfa. Called Medice by the Greeks for the lush valleys of Media where it grew wild, alfalfa was first introduced to Greece when the Persians under Darius I carried it there as fodder.

Unlike the Greeks and Romans, the Persians had no early historians, and we learn much of their history from their adversaries. The sacred literature of the Zoroastrians was recorded during Sassanian rule 200–635 A.D., but the legends of the kings written during this era were more heroic myth than actual history. The first detailed descriptions of the Sassanian Empire were those of later Arab geographers. The earliest accounts are the Arab Road Books of the ninth century, which were essentially "Guide Books" for the convenience of Muslim pilgrims, giving stage by stage itineraries with useful notes on cities. Such guides were necessary because it was not only his heart's desire but the duty of a devout Muslim to make the pilgrimage to Mecca.[3]

Beginning in the tenth century, systematic geographies and histories of the provinces of the Muslim Empire were assembled. From this time on, the number of descriptive and historic works by scholars and travelers increased, and the Persian past can be pieced together. These writers were the source for Edward Gibbon, whose references to the Persian Empire were most influential in forming the exotic notion of Persia so common in the West. There was always a great lag between European knowledge and the reality of life behind the silken curtain which screened the East. The Venetian merchant, Marco Polo (1254–1324), the first European to traverse and record the route across Asia, added much accurate information to knowledge about the East. His most important record may have been of his sea voyage to India from China. Originally transcribed in French in 1298–1299, his *Travels* were not widely accepted in France and not translated into English until 1579, centuries after the second Mongol invasion had ground to dust much of the splendor and many of the gardens he described.

The early Arab authorities frequently mention qanat lines, cisterns for water storage, irrigated gardens and palm groves in the settlements of domed houses they found throughout Iran. They refer to the palaces of the Sassanid Dynasty with awe, overwhelmed by their grandeur, finding the great arches remarkable. In fact, these writers resorted to the fabulous in their descriptions with references to "fathomless tanks" and "bottomless pools."

The Sassanian rulers apparently wished to appear in history as colossi judging from the monumental pictorial record they left carved on rock cliffs throughout eastern Iran. Similar reliefs and proclamations were carved by the Achaemenians and Medes, but were an even older tradition. In the Zagros Mountains, panels portraying victorious kings and defeated prisoners date from the twentieth century B.C.—perhaps even earlier.

The Sassanians, like the Achaemenians, originated in the province of Fars. Their rockcut panels, mostly found there, glorify the king, who is often shown to be twice the size of other men and victorious in mounted combat. These reliefs appear on the sheer face of cliffs usually above a spring or stream, and they often mark the approach to huge Sassanian palaces or to a Pairidaeza.

Obviously colorful, active men, the Sassanian rulers, with their puffy hair styles and billowing trousers, were proud of their prowess as hunters and their skill with the bow. Rather than palace court gardens, they seem to have preferred the Achaemenid Pairidaeza which they maintained as vast hunting parks.

The Sassanians revived Zoroastrianism. During their era there was widespread worship of an ancient water cult which influenced their building. From existing ruins it appears that these kings preferred to place their palaces overlooking pools fed by natural springs. Within the ruins of several massive Sassanian palaces some stucco-lined pools fed by water conduits of clay pipes have been found. Similar interior pools are common in later Persian architecture.

What remains of the palace of the first Sassanian warrior-king, Ardashir I (226–240) stands deserted on the Plain of Firuzabad in Fars. The crumbling 13-foot thick walls of the 340-feet long palace stretch away behind a spring-fed, circular pool, the only relic of the garden.

In writing of Firuzabad, the Arab geographers tell a local legend of a lake created by Alexander who diverted the river and flooded the plain. Drained later by King Ardashir I, the plain was instantly famous for the red roses which sprang up there. The local attar of roses was exported to India, China, Egypt, and the Maghrib. The area around Firuzabad had also a profitable trade in palm flower water and perfumes distilled from southernwood, saffron, lily, and willow flowers.

Takht-i Suleiman showing crater lake, ruins and fortifications of cone. (Courtesy of the Oriental Institute, University of Chicago)

Other valleys in Fars exported aromatic grains which grew wild, and several had a worldwide commerce in perfumed oils or unguents made from violet, water-lily, narcissus, jasmine, myrtle, sweet marjoram, lemon and orange flowers.[4]

Ardashir I was known to have worshipped in Istakhr at a temple dedicated to the water goddess Anahita where his grandfather, Sasan, served as high priest. The goddess personified the cosmic spring, the source of all water. Also referred to as the fountain goddess, Anahita is usually depicted holding a symbolic vase from which flow the waters of life.

The water goddess was an ancient and widespread symbol, identified with Nanaia in Mesopotamia and with Aphrodite or Artemis in Greece. Goddesses with flowing vases were worshipped in ancient India. The cult of Anahita had grown strong under the later Achaemenians, and remained popular throughout the Sassanian era. Fire temples dedicated to her have been found in several sanctuaries in Iran. Under Sassanian rule, where Zoroastrianism was the state religion, the fire temples became centers of teaching as well as rites. This was a period of intense religious sentiment. Professor Richard Frye writes that Zoroastrian heresies, as well as foreign religions, had been intermittently attacked during the reign of early Sassanian kings, but the first great persecution of Christians in the Persian Empire occurred under Shapur II beginning about 339 A.D.[5]

As early as 334 A.D., Christian monasteries were built in the Sassanian Empire. Writing in the tenth century, the Arab historian, Shabusti, described the old monastery of Marmi "sixteen leagues from Baghdad." Within high, fortress-like walls the one hundred cells had adjoining gardens, each watered by a small canal and planted with fruit trees.

During his seventy-year reign (310–379), Shapur II built a sanctuary dedicated to the water goddess Anahita; although famous for its splendor, the exact location of the sanctuary was unknown for centuries. Now, the site of the sanctuary may have been identified. In a remote and fertile valley in the mountains of Azerbaijan, a strange hill rises with an almost circular crater-like lake on its level summit. The plateau is known as Takht-i-Suleiman and is the site of the ancient holy Zoroastrian city of Shiz. Excavations, begun in 1957 by Dr. Rudolph Naumann, revealed a large fire temple and other buildings buried under masses of rubble and debris. There is evidence that Shiz was a Zoroastrian site as early as Achaemenid times and had been an earlier sacred site of the Medes. Several ceremonial buildings of Parthian or Sassanian origin have been excavated. Later Islamic palaces were constructed over some of these earlier temples, and the plateau fortified.

The plateau with the lake is a unique natural phenomenon. The hill rises sixty meters and was formed by deposits of calciferous sediment from the extraordinarily deep springs which created the lake. Such an unusual natural setting would have been a stunning site for the sanctuary of the "moist and mighty and undefiled" water goddess, Ardvi Sura Anahita.

In his book, *Paradisus Terrestris*, Lars Ivar Ringbom concluded that Shapur's sanctuary was in a Pairidaeza encircling Anahita's fountain and that it was at Takht-i-Suleiman. He believes that a Sassanian salver, in the Staatliche Museen in Berlin, represents this Pairidaeza, though this interpretation of the salver is disputed by other scholars. Dr. Ringbom's comments on the decoration are important. He interpreted the repeated arcade of spiral columns supporting pearled arches as "more than mere decoration: it indicated, I believe, the outer

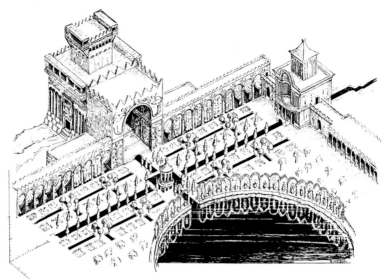

Conjectural drawing of sacred buildings at Shiz with pairidaeza, based on interpretation of the site by L. I. Ringbom.

wall of a paridaeza garden." Dr. Ringbom pointed out the similarity of these Sassanian architectural details to early Christian motifs: "We find this arcade motif on reliquaries and sarcophagi almost everywhere in Antiquity, from India to Gaul." He quotes the scholar Benjamin Rowland, Jr., who described the arcade as a "means of representing the architecture of Paradise." Dr. Ringbom concurs, "The arcade design on an Iranian ossuary, and that on a Christian sarcophagus were basically reflections of the same idea: the beautiful architecture in a transcendent Paradise."[6]

If Dr. Ringbom is correct, the salver is an example of the elegant arcaded wall surrounding a sacred Sassanian Pairidaeza. It provides a beautiful setting for the joyful celebration honoring Anahita with lithe ritual dancers and graceful animals, with symbolic flowers and vines. In the hypothetical drawing included by Dr. Ringbom, the garden is divided by crossed watercourses lined with cypress trees.

During the Sassanian era, architecture of royal buildings and gardens continued to contribute to the glorification of the Persian king by providing an unmatched, formal setting for the supreme monarch. The dazzling Sassanian court had strict rules of precedence and absurd protocol: a long transparent curtain, encrusted with precious jewels and embroidered with gold and silver, hung in the throne hall between the king and his petitioners.

Perhaps the greatest Sassanian king, the strong and reform-minded Khusrau I (531–579), ruled from a winter capital at Ctesiphon on the Tigris. Visitors to his Throne Hall have provided what is probably the earliest record of the design of a Sassanian garden by their description of his great garden carpet. The awesome span of the parabolic vault of the audience hall arched 110 feet above a marble-paved floor, covered with the costliest and most splendid carpet ever made.[7] Sections of heavy woven silk were joined together to create a carpet 84 feet square worked with gold and precious jewels. Called the "Spring of Khusrau" or

Sassanian bronze salver with water goddess surrounded by symbols: flowing scarf, peacocks, flowing vase. (Hermitage Museum)

the "Winter Carpet," it portrayed the perfection of a formal garden caught forever in the loveliness of an eternal spring. This fabulous carpet was said to have been the design of an actual royal garden.

Arthur Upham Pope, drawing on eyewitness accounts, has described the carpet: "The ground of the carpet represented a beautiful pleasure garden with running brooks and interlacing paths, adorned with trees and lovely spring flowers. The wide borders surrounding it represented beautifully planted flower beds in manifold colours: blue, red, yellow, white, and green precious stones which portrayed the beauty of the flowers. The yellow soil was imitated in gold as were the banks of the brooks; crystal clear stones represented the rippling water. The gravel paths were imitated in stones the size of pearls. The trunks and branches of the trees were of gold and silver; the leaves of the trees and the flowers and plants were of silk and the fruits of many-coloured stones. According to another description, there was an outer border of solid emeralds representing a meadow or grassy field."

Never equalled, this splendid creation served as a model for garden carpets for a thousand years. All of these carpets illustrate a walled garden outlined by trees and feature a boldly designed central watercourse with one or more cross channels bordered by paths and multi-colored flower plots. The basic design was consistent, though details varied: geometric flower beds, colorful birds, and amusing fish swimming in channels and pools. Though actual gardens apparently were copied for some carpets, the designers of many of the best carpets aspired to reproduce the perfect garden—Paradise.[8]

The "Winter Carpet" not only charmed the king as a constant reminder of Paradise; it provided a majestic setting which overwhelmed visitors to the court. In his magnificent throne room, Khusrau I graciously received seven Athenian philosophers who fled from the Roman Emperor Justinian when he closed the

33

Garden carpet. Iran, *ca.* 1790. (Courtesy of the Fogg Art Museum, Harvard University. Gift of Joseph V. McMullan)

School of Athens in 529 A.D. Khusrau I had established a school of philosophy and medicine and had the works of Plato and Aristotle translated from the Greek. However, the Athenian philosophers found Khusrau more Oriental and less enlightened than they had hoped; disliking the sumptuous Persian court life, they returned to Athens.

Though a disappointment to the Greek thinkers, Khusrau I was a popular king. As part of his policy of improving agriculture, he initiated programs of land reclamation, distribution of seeds, and instruction for peasants in better methods of farming. Bridges, dams, and aqueducts from the expanded irrigation systems that the Sassanians constructed remain throughout Persia.

Khusrau's spectacular carpet was captured when the Arabs took Ctesiphon in the next century (635). Scornful of the display of royal luxury and power, they cut it into fragments. One fifth went to the Caliph, Omar, one piece to the Prophet's son-in-law Ali, and the rest was divided among 60,000 warriors.[9]

The Sassanian kings were able to satisfy their characteristic Persian longing for spring by these great carpets they spread beneath their golden thrones. The floor of another famous Throne Hall, that of Khusrau II (591–628), was said to be spread with four different carpets every day of the month, each representing one season of the year. Some experts believe that this Throne Hall was located near the sanctuary of Anahita overlooking the crater lake at Takht-i-Suleiman.

While still a prince, Khusrau II served as governor of Kirmanshah in western Iran where he chose a dramatic site for an unusual Pairidaeza. At Taq-i Bustan (Arch of the Garden), the acres of garden fell away toward the plain beneath the last outcropping of a line of craggy hills. Though most of the cultivated area of the Pairidaeza has disappeared, two grottos, carved into the steep rock face remain, the last rock-carving of the Sassanians. The larger grotto, thirty feet high and twenty-one feet deep, is dedicated to Khusrau II. One panel records the investiture of the king; to his right is the goddess Anahita. This panel gives the appearance of being supported by two columns representing the cosmological tree. Carved as pilasters, they are crowned by growing, fanciful flowers. A spring flows from the mountain and fills the pool in front of the sculpted grottos.

The side panels of the larger grotto consist of the famous chase panels. They are carved in a lower relief than most Sassanian panels, rather more like metalwork technique than that of stone. The carvings do not reveal the design of the Pairidaeza, but do show details of a royal hunt, such as might have taken place here, therefore illustrating the use of a Pairidaeza by the Sassanians.

In one chase scene, the action takes place within an enclosure created by huge cloth panels staked and tied to regularly spaced trees. Well-modeled elephants slog through the rushes to drive wild boar toward the king who is shown in gorgeous dress—a gigantic figure standing stiffly in a boat. Other boats carry women harpists, attendants, and musicians. Frenzied fish, placid ducks, straining huntsmen and crashing boars fill the remainder of the panel. The Sassanians seem to have had a zest for life; certainly in these panels, the pageantry reveals that the chase was probably more important than the kill.

The scale on which Persian royalty lived was stupendous, as Edward Gibbon indicated in a description of the principal summer palace of the king: "Its paradise, or park, was replenished with pheasants, peacocks, ostriches, roe bucks and wild boar, and the noble game of lions and tigers was sometimes turned

Taq-i Bustan. Grottoes carved into base of crag above greatly foreshortened pairidaeza. (Courtesy of the Oriental Institute, University of Chicago)

loose, for the bolder pleasures of the chase. Nine hundred-sixty elephants were maintained for the use of the great king." [10]

Star-crossed lovers were always a favorite theme of Persian poets. Written by Nizami in the twelfth century, one popular poem recalls the romance of Khusrau II who loved the beautiful Armenian princess, Shirin. Taq-i Bustan was the setting for part of this romance so frequently illustrated by miniaturists. But as the painters strove to create a mood rather than a faithful representation of the scene, their works should not be considered an accurate portrayal of the garden.

Many visitors have made their way to the ruins of the isolated retreat of the legendary royal lovers, Khusrau II and Shirin. At Qasr-i-Shirin in the western foothills of the Zagros mountains where the ancient route crossed from the sandy plains up to Ecbatana, near the beginning of the seventh century Khusrau II built a palace for Shirin enclosed in the center of a 300-acre "King's Paradise Park."

The decaying walls of the palace in the center of the garden are of sandstone rubble crudely set in rough mortar; the collapsed stone dome was the largest ever raised by the Sassanians. In 1812, C. J. Rich, the East India Company's resident in Baghdad who made such careful measurements of sites along the Tigris and detailed maps of Kurdistan, visited the palace of Khusrau and left unimpressed. A village had grown up in the arcades beneath the long palace terrace and it was difficult, even for his discerning eye, to make out the plan. The narrow 1,800-feet long pool which lay between the palace and the gate had filled up and was being cultivated. He noticed sections of an old aqueduct on the

36

hillside, which must have been the remains of the original which encircled the entire Pairidaeza.[11]

The decline and defeat of the Sassanians came suddenly. Khusrau II over-taxed his country, and a series of wars with Rome depleted Persian resources. In 636 the Arabs defeated the Persian army and by 642 they had overrun the entire empire.

For centuries after the Arab conquest, Sassanian design influenced weaving, pottery, and metalwork. Based on older Persian traditions, Sassanian architecture, larger than it was lovely, was nevertheless powerful and proved to have a strong influence on later building. They made wide use of the *squinch*, a simple arch across the angle of two walls, to raise a round dome on a square base—the solution to what had been a great architectural puzzle. The heroic scale of their building construction of arches without centering, necessary in areas with little wood available, was made possible through the use of fast-setting gypsum mortar. The great arched entrance to Sassanian courts or audience halls inspired the deeply vaulted *iwan*, or portal, characteristic of the four-iwan court of Iranian mosques, and used throughout the Islamic world. An adaptation of the iwans was used with great effect by the later Mughal emperors of India to mark the entrance to their walled Paradise gardens.

Shirin visiting Farhad where he was carving figures on mountain. Timurid, 1481. (Chester Beatty Library, Dublin)

37

THREE

The Arabs:
Islam

The Arab horsemen who burst out of the desert in the seventh century and quickly overran the Persian Empire influenced Persian life more fundamentally than any previous conquerors. Though the Persians rose to rule again, the Arab legacy was permanent: Persians remained adherents of Islam.

In discussing the effect of the astonishing speed of the Arab victories, H. A. R. Gibb expressed the view that this confirmed Islam's self-confidence and unyielding attitude toward everything outside itself. At the same time, he wrote: "To the peoples of the conquered countries the Arab supremacy signified at first little more than a change of masters. There was no breach in the continuity of their life and social institutions, no persecutions, no forced conversion. But little by little Islam began to modify the old social structure of western Asia and Egypt, and Arab elements to penetrate the old Persian and Hellenistic cultures."[1]

In Persia, the moral force of the zealous Arab onslaught almost extinguished the holy fires of the Zoroastrians. The first Sassanian king, Ardashir I, had been an ardent believer who made Zoroastrianism the state religion and strengthened the Magi, or priesthood. His successors lacked the tolerance of the Achaemenians and, protected by the kings, the Magi gained great power and forced strict compliance with holy law. Under Arab rule, many Persians converted from the ancient creed of their prophet, Zoroaster, to the new simpler, monotheistic creed of Mohammed. Others, resisting forced conversion, fled to India along the trade routes following the coast. Once settled in India, these Zoroastrians established the *Parsi* community, the name being derived from "Persia." Other Zoroastrians, like the last king's son, sought sanctuary in China. In the eighth century, Persian quarters with their fire temples existed in several Chinese cities.[2]

The ruins of Zoroastrian fire temples still dot hilltops in Iran where for centuries they also served as beacons for caravans. The holy eternal fires burned on, quietly tended by a handful of Zoroastrians in a few remote cities skirting the desert.

In their rapid rise to power, the Arabs brought little with them beyond their calligraphy and their creed. The rich and fabled ancient kingdoms of southern

Arabia had depended on trade and irrigation for their prosperity. When sea routes for the spice trade between India and Egypt were established, the importance of the Arabian oasis cities along the land route was diminished. With the destruction of ancient dams and the irrigation systems of Arabia Deserta, its cities disappeared, and its civilization was all but unknown to the Arabs of the Prophet's time.

Lacking a strong cultural tradition of their own, the Arabs showed a genius for absorbing those of the countries they conquered and, developing an integrated Islamic style. Much of this Islamic style, including the garden tradition, was taken from the established Persian civilization.

The early Arab Muslims were simple men accustomed to a wide horizon and open sky. They had mastered the desert with their camels and had mastered the sea as skillful sailors. Green, the color of vegetation, was a sacred color to these desert men. Though it is not surprising that they would be attracted to Persian gardens, there is a certain incongruity in picturing these austere Arabs, with their contempt for death, reposing in felicitous gardens contemplating limpid pools. The Koran, however, promises entrance to the Garden of Paradise to anyone slain fighting for the "Way of God." The Koranic Paradise, the abiding mansion, is watered by rivers, and there are repeated promises of shade and fountains: "There shall be two other gardens: of a dark green. In each of them shall be two fountains pouring forth plenty of water. In each of them shall be fruits and palm trees and pomegranates. Therein shall be agreeable and beauteous damsels."[3] In the Koran, the wives of perfect purity, and promised, black-eyed maidens recline on green silken cushions and beautiful carpets in cool pavilions. This Paradise, a series of walled gardens, is Allah's reward to god-fearing men and women, the humble and the almsgivers, the forgiving and those who have suffered for God's sake.

Though the absolute monotheism of Islam rejected nature cults and, therefore, some of the symbolism attached to gardens, the Muslims found the Persian garden the earthly counterpart of the promised Koranic Paradise. The space of the Persian garden, as precisely defined by its watercourse, reflected the cosmic order of an ordered universe which existed according to divine law. To them it seemed the physical expression of the mystical relationship of a garden to Paradise; the essence of this relationship was strikingly represented in the use of water—life-giving, life-sustaining, purifying water.

Within the protective walls of a garden, in the privacy of a man-made paradisal oasis, the sensual pleasures could be enjoyed—a foretaste of the promised eternal Paradise. The admiration of the garden must be considered in itself an act of piety for within its walls the transformation of barren earth into fruitful orchards through water was evidence of God's power of creation.

The early Arab Caliphs governed like tribal leaders. However, while Arabic was the official language, the clever and culturally superior Persians proved indispensable in administration. Following a sectarian Muslim struggle for succession in 750, the Abbasid family gained the Caliphate with Persian support. There followed the zenith of the Islamic Caliphate with Persian cultural influence dominant.

Stones from the Sassanian capital of Ctesiphon were dragged twenty miles and used in the palace of the Abbasid Caliph in his new, circular city of Baghdad

Jerusalem. Dome of the Rock, 691.
Floral motif is similar to the
Sassanian tree of life. See note 4,
Chapter Three.

which adorned the west bank of the Tigris. Workmen from throughout Islam were required for the vast four-year project, but the architects and master builders were Persian. Baghdad became the leading intellectual and commercial capital of the Islamic world. The remains of the Abbasid capital lie beneath the modern city of Baghdad; as no scientific excavation is possible, literary references are almost the only source of information about its appearance. At the beginning of the ninth century, Baghdad was reputed to be the wealthiest city in the world, famous for its tiled buildings and its houses with gardens and pools. It was the fairy-tale city of *Arabian Nights*. Tenth-century visitors describe the palace as having two gardens, pools lined with shiny tin, and pavilions with gilt seats. "All round this tank extended a garden with lawns with palm trees, and it is said that their number was four hundred, and the height of each was five cubits."

The Arabs had maintained the existing Persian canal systems, so the Euphrates River basin had remained well-populated and prosperous, but the survival of Asian cities is precariously linked to religious and political movements and the capricious whims of rulers. Thus, Baghdad declined when abandoned by the Caliph Mutasim (833–842) who built a new city at Samarra.

Before building his palace at Samarra, Mutasim constructed a system of waterways and planted groves of date palms with an irrigation network. Spread over four hundred acres, of which 172 were gardens, the Jawsaq palace had vaulted halls, extensive quarters for a large harem and luxurious private quarters for the king. The largest palace ever constructed in the Islamic world and occupied for only a few years, it was built of unbaked brick with a flat mud roof and quickly became a ruin when abandoned. The remains reveal chambers decorated with murals and built around courts with fountains and aromatic plants. In describing these murals, Richard Ettinghausen wrote: "The Persian character of these pictures calls to mind a story in the *Arabian Nights* according to which the paintings in a garden pavilion were executed in the Persian manner by several Persian painters whom the caliph had called in for this purpose."[5] Arab historians describe a large garden on the opposite bank of the river linked to the palace by a bridge of boats. For this garden, the Caliph imported plants from all corners of the empire.

The early Caliphs enjoyed hunting. Like the Sassanian kings, in pursuit of this pleasure, they built palaces as hunting lodges and Pairidaeza near extensive royal hunting grounds. So we learn that the Arab conquerors had succumbed to the charms of the Persian garden and absorbed them into the new Islamic culture. The tradition of the enclosed Persian garden with its crossed watercourse and symbolic trees spread with Islam throughout Egypt and the Maghrib, to Sicily and Spain.[6] Though many of these states declared their independence of the central Caliphate, and the empire was politically fragmented, Islamic culture flourished during this period.

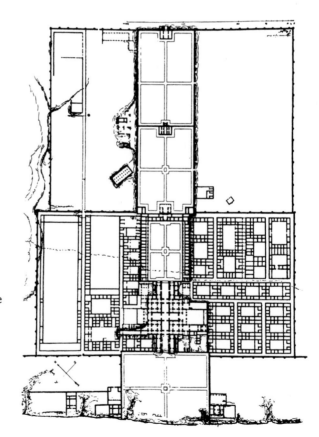

Samarra. Bulkawara Palace, 849–859. Of the palace J. D. Hoag has written: "Beside the river a quadripartite garden flanked by pavilions overlooking the water was probably an intentional evocation of the Koran's paradise suggested also by the mosaic vines of the nearby portal."

John D. Hoag, *Western Islamic Architecture* (New York: 1963) p.18.

41

Sicily, 1134. Coronation robe of Roger II. Palm tree (center) designated royalty in the ancient Near East. Arabic inscription embroidered on the hem refers to "pleasures of days and nights without surcease and change." (Kunsthistorische Museum, Vienna)

Ahmad Ibn Tulun, who was raised at the court in Samarra, established the independent Tulunid Dynasty after he was appointed governor of Egypt in 869. As John Hoag has stated, "His mosque, finished in 879, introduced Cairo to several new ideas from Samarra."[7] Chief among these ideas was the spiral *minaret* similar to the curious freestanding minaret wrapped in a winding ramp at the great mosque at Samarra, begun in 847. The Sultan's palace included gardens similar to those of Samarra with pools like those of Baghdad. According to Marie L. Gotheim in her *History of Garden Art,* saffron was included in the Tulunid gardens, thus introducing it to Egypt. In contrast to the Persian practice of allowing natural growth, she claims that under the Tulunids, "Their gardeners cut plants into various figures, as well as the shapes of letters, and this had to be kept up regularly, lest a single leaf should stick out."[8]

The Arabs captured Palermo in 831 and introduced the sour orange to Sicily in the gardens they built there: a small, water-loving tree, its fragrant flowers belie its bitter fruit. In addition to its abundant blossoms, the sour orange produced a valuable crop and was, therefore, an incomparably important tree in the gardens and orchards of the Persians since its introduction from southeast Asia, probably southern Vietnam, much earlier. By 965, the Arabs controlled all of Sicily and built splendid villas and Pairidaezas, which were captured by the Normans almost two hundred-fifty years later when, with Papal support, they took the island.

The Norman kings of Sicily adopted many Muslim ways including the wide use of Arabic and built their palaces in the Saracenic style.[9] One of the many gardens built by Roger the Great on the outskirts of Palermo was a Pairidaeza which was said to cover two miles with groves of trees, luxurious gardens, pools, and pavilions. In the fifteenth century some gardens remained at La Cuba and the Castle of Zisa. In his *Travels* in 1526, Alberti described the romantic ruins of one royal garden where the palace overlooked a pool, fifty feet square, fed by a watercourse from the main hall. The pool was faced with stone, and a stone bridge led to a square pavilion in the center. The surroundings, he said, were "Beautiful gardens filled with orange and lime trees and exotic shrubs." Early nineteenth-century drawings show the waterchannel in the Castle of Zisa to be in the familiar ancient Persian style with regularly spaced square basins.[10]

As the capital of Moorish Spain after 756, Cordova had a distinctive architecture with celebrated palaces and gardens. Though greatly rebuilt through the centuries, the Generalife and Alhambra in Granada still contain widely admired old gardens. The most familiar, the Court of the Lions in the Alhambra, is a classic Persian palace garden with a crossed watercourse and four plots which originally held aromatic plants and flowers.[11] The lion fountains in the center are reminiscent of the sculptural treatment of lions by the Achaemenids.[12] The arcaded walk surrounding the court reminds many Western visitors of the cloisters of medieval monasteries which derive from the peristyle of Roman villas. Monastery gardens and cemeteries were occasionally referred to as Paradise, but not their cloisters.

Paradoxically, in Persia, the garden came to be both a reminder of mortality and a symbol of eternity. This paradox, which so appealed to the poetic nature of the Persians, was studied by religious mystics. The *Sufis*, or mystics, were also fascinated by the parallelism between man and nature. In commenting on this, Anne Marie Schimmel has written: "The Sufis, generally endowed with a poetical mind and artistic perception, were fond of discovering analogies between the different aspects of creation; thus it is small wonder that they very early began to ponder the relationship of man and nature, and soon discovered a basic similarity between man's behavior and the state of the garden. Did not even the Koran

The Prophet's Tree of Bliss in Paradise which grew downwards toward the earth. Turkish prayer book, eighteenth century. (Chester Beatty Library, Dublin)

prove the possibility of man's resurrection by examples taken from nature? As the dead earth will be resurrected in spring to be adorned with lovely green sprouts and flowers, the dead bones which were apparently rotten under the dust will be quickened again at Doomsday."[13]

Within their gardens, the Persians indulged their passion for poetry, which equalled their passion for flowers. They preferred to spend their evenings in a garden, in the company of friends, reclining on carpets in a pavilion. Enveloped by the perfume of flowers and listening for the song of the nightingale, the Persians recited poetry to the accompanying sound of rippling water.

This use of the garden was equally attractive to the Arabs, with their oral tradition of storytelling and their *qasida* or odes with identical rhymes. Developed by the pre-Islamic Bedouin tribes, the qasida's themes reflected the fundamental nature of their lives in the Arabian desert. Combining the poetic and oral traditions of the Persians and the Arabs, the poetry which flourished in Islamic Persia was rich in garden imagery, much of it linking the garden to Paradise.

The greatest epic in Persian literature, the *Shah-Nama* or Book of Kings, an idealized history of the Persian kings, was completed about 1010 by the poet Abu l-Qasim, who adopted the name "Firdausi," meaning of the garden or Paradise. References to the Koranic Paradise, and floral and garden imagery expressed in charming descriptions, abound in the long epic. "Her cheeks were as red as pomegranate blossoms and her lips like its seeds, while two pomegranates grew from her silver breasts. Her eyes were like the narcissus in the garden, and her eyebrows stole the blackness from the crow's features. She is a Paradise to look upon."[14]

The still-popular poet Sa'di (1184–1291) used garden imagery to such an extent that he even named two of his most widely read books *Gulistan*, meaning rose garden, and *Bustan*, meaning fruit garden or orchard. After the destructive Mongol invasion of Persia, Sa'di spent thirty years wandering and did not return to his native Shiraz until 1256 when he was over 70. Shiraz, in Fars, has always claimed to be the city of roses and nightingales, wine and poetry. In a custom unchanged through the centuries, Shirazis still gather informally on holidays in the tomb garden of Sa'di and that of the great lyrical poet Hafiz (*ca.* 1300–1389). Hafiz, whose poetry contains some of the most powerful and evocative descriptions of nature, chose to be buried in his own much-loved garden. The countless

Detail from the Book of Antidotes of Pseudo-Galen, 1199. (Bibliothèque Nationale Paris)

44

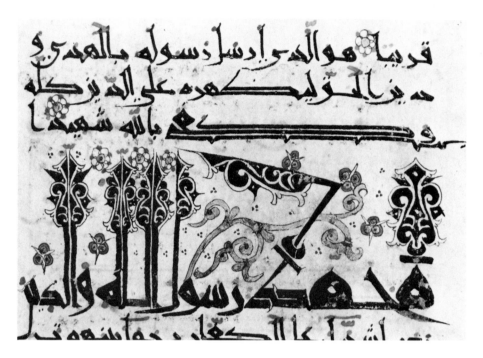

Iran, eleventh century. Koran leaf in foliated Kufic script. (Courtesy of the Metropolitan Museum of Art, Rogers Fund)

images in Persian poetry illustrate a deep feeling for gardens; abstract and idealized, however, they are not descriptions of actual gardens.

Though the Arabs adopted many Persian traditions, they contributed to Persian culture as well. Calligraphy was a truly Arabic art, the most respected skill in the Islamic world. Indeed, the development of written Arabic was very closely identified with the Koran. Paper was unknown and unavailable to the companions of the Prophet, so they copied his inspired discourses on any material available. After his death his words were collected into one volume, the first book known in the Arabic language—the Koran. Quotations from the Koran became the chief decoration for mosques, and the perfection of the script became a high art. The Persians excelled in producing imaginative variations of Arabic script.

Somewhere near the close of the eighth century, the Muslims fearing idolatry had introduced a ban against the portrayal of animal or human figures. This was not an obstacle for the talented Persians; their gift for decoration and love of flowers combined to produce some of the most wonderful stylized vegetation. There were vines, blossoms, fanciful flowers, and buds and leaves curling, swirling, interweaving, and twining into the most ingenious and beautiful running patterns. They were painted, carved, inlaid, and woven on every imaginable surface. The foliate decoration which appears free, is actually contained within a defined geometric space to adhere to the Islamic principles of an ordered world.

FOUR

The Central Asians: Submission

As the chill winds and driving rain of an unexpected storm can destroy a delicate spring garden, the raids by the wandering tribes of the north of Asia all but ended the flourishing civilization of Persia. Centralized rule had been greatly weakened with the decline of the Caliphate, and local dynasties had gained independence. Commencing in the eleventh century, power was gained and rule established by dynasties descended from Turkish-speaking Central Asian no-mads. Even so, continual raids by Turkoman tribes destroyed irrigation systems and depopulated the countryside in eastern Iran in the twelfth century.

It was common practice for raiding parties of Central Asians to fill their enemies' wells with sand. Productive agricultural land became pasture; the gradual nomadization which resulted was accelerated by the first Mongol inva-sions in 1218 when Jenghiz Khan, leading his horde of mounted bowmen, rode out of the East. His army pillaged and plundered the cities of what is now Afghanistan and eastern Iran. The long-haired barbarians destroyed crops and with them the prosperity of the area. The systematic destruction of irrigation systems made recovery difficult or impossible and entire regions were turned into desert. Dozens of cities were left to lie in ruins where they had stood in glory; some vanished without a trace only to be unearthed in this century. Professor M. Tosi, who has directed some of the archaeological excavations in Sistan, eastern Iran, describes it as "the country of Dead Cities."[1]

The western areas of the empire did not escape the devastation. In 1258 Hulagu, grandson of Jenghiz Khan, attacked Baghdad, massacred the people, and destroyed the irrigation system by breaking down the banks of the canals. His vandalism created malarial swamps and brought disease and famine, ruining the fertile land. In one raid, he caused more ecological damage than had occurred from thousands of years of irrigation and constant use.

After taking Herat in 1381, Timur—another Central Asian—swept unopposed with his horde across Persia wielding his bloody sword. A vengeful and unpre-dictable victor, he sometimes spared buildings but slaughtered the population.

This simultaneous disruption of the eastern and western trade routes on the

Iranian plateau resulted in a change in the economic base in Persia, and poverty and misery took root in areas that once were prosperous. Near the close of the eleventh century, there was a revival in Persia of the Ismaili sect, followers of the independent Fatamid Caliph of Cairo. Their strength grew through the bizarre activities of the secret branch of the sect known as the *Assassins.* The proper term for them, *Hashishin,* means taker of hashish; at the time it was believed that they were fanatic murderers who performed their evil deeds while under the effects of the drug. Their notoriety caused fear to spread throughout much of the world; in time the name, *Assassin,* came into general use, meaning secret professional murderer.

Firmly established in a network of impregnable mountain strongholds, they were finally routed by Hulagu Khan in 1256 when he captured their last Grand Master, or Old Man of the Mountain, at Alamut. The colorful description of the Master's methods and castle, written by Marco Polo, is apparently apocryphal, but it was widely believed:

> The Old Man was called in their language *ALOADIN.* He had caused a certain valley between two mountains to be enclosed, and had turned it into a garden, the largest and most beautiful that ever was seen, filled with every variety of fruit. In it was erected pavilions and palaces, the most elegant that can be imagined, all covered with gilding and exquisite painting. And there were runnels, too, flowing freely with wine and milk and honey and water; and numbers of ladies and of the most beautiful damsels in the world, who could play on all manner of instruments, and sung most sweetly, and danced in a manner that it was charming to behold. For the Old Man desired to make his people believe that this was actually Paradise. So he had fashioned it after the description that Mahommet gave of his Paradise.[2]

The lengthy account describes how the Old Man would drug his recruits who awoke in his garden and believed they were in Paradise—where they "dallied" with beautiful damsels "to their hearts content." When assassins were needed to slay a prince, the Old Man would drug them and return them to the Castle. He knew he could count on their fanatic dedication to his mission, that "there was no order of his that they would not affront any peril to execute, for the great desire they had to get back into that Paradise of his."

Historically, the artistic traditions of Persia had been aristocratic, and artists depended on the courts for patronage. Under the Central Asians brilliant courts were maintained, and the arts flourished though the plight of the population was pitiful. E. J. W. Gibb gives an explanation for the paradox of these violent tribesmen as patrons of the arts: "That great race . . . . which includes not only the Turks both western and eastern, but all the so-called Tartars and Turkomans, as well as the Mongols, has never produced any religion, philosophy or literature which bears the stamp of its individual genius. This is because the true genius of the race lies in action, not in speculation . . . . Consequently, when brought into close connection with the Persians, although they despised the latter as men, looking upon them as braggarts and cowards, they at once recognized their superiority in learning and culture."[3]

The Ilkhans, the thirteenth-century descendants of Jenghiz Khan, who had converted to Islam, were great patrons of painting; a distinctive style developed

47

Temptation in the Garden of Paradise from
Chronology of Ancient Peoples, 1307–1308.
(Edinburgh Library)

Love Scene by Ustad Muhammadi, *ca.* 1575.
(Courtesy, Museum of Fine Arts, Boston. Frances
Bartlett Donation)

at their court in Tabriz. As Persian painting matured, the genius of the painters was displayed in their individual ability to interpret favorite scenes within a rigid framework. The Islamic ban against figural representation did not inhibit the painters, for people were their main subject. Though the heroic accounts of the lives of kings and the epic poems were the manuscripts most frequently illustrated, the people in them were pictured in very human situations. In the paintings, which are rich with detail, the mood was created by contrasts in color balanced within the whole composition. Painted with frequent wit and drama, the figures are to the viewer what actors are to an audience. The wonderful clarity of the color in Persian paintings was achieved through the use of mineral pigments of exceptionally high quality found locally.

Gardens, a favorite theme and setting in the paintings, were not portrayals of actual gardens but most frequently were idealized scenes capturing the perfection of springtime with fruit blossoms and spring flowers. In a Persian garden, dense shade, providing protection from the relentless sun, was one of the most desirable features, but Persian paintings were particularly characterized by the lack of shadows. Some plants took on added symbolism; the familiar intertwining cypress and peach trees often represented lovers. The delicate, short-lived peach had a poignant appeal and was a favorite of painters, as well as gardeners.

The Ilkhans also introduced new plants, such as the peony, into Persian gardens. After Kublai, the son of Jenghiz Khan, became the Great Khan of Cathay, Chinese influence flowered in Mongol culture. The single, white or pink peony grew wild in China and had been cultivated for centuries by the Chinese who developed double varieties in a wide range of shades. Though not unknown to the Persians, under the Ilkhans the peony became a dominant flower in Persian decoration frequently found on carpets, in textiles and a favorite flower in gardens.

During the ascendancy of the Turkish-speaking rulers the use of the word *bagh,* meaning garden, apparently came into common usage. The etymology of bagh is difficult to trace; thought to be an ancient Persian word known to the Achaemenians, it appears in mid-Persian and was used by the Sassanians. In Central Asia, the area of Samarkand and Bukhara, it was evidently a common word for gardens. Bagh reappeared in general use in Persia after the conquest by the Central Asians. With the prefix *chahar,* meaning four, the term *chaharbagh* was commonly used to mean a four-fold, enclosed garden.

Except for the hunting parks, it seems the Persians continued their sedentary use of the gardens. It was frequently noted that Persians seldom walked in their gardens; rather, they preferred to observe them from an open pavilion or a raised, recessed platform of the house, much like the ca. fifth-century B.C. pavilions of Cyrus at Pasargadae.

Though the Turkish-speaking tribes of the east and west adopted the Persian tradition of the garden, they extended its use and design. Simply put, it was a change from inactive to active use; from a mere background or place to observe idealized nature, the garden became a place for activities. This functional change led to the expansion of the conventional garden design. The gardens built by the nomadic Central Asians combined features of the Pairidaeza with the design of palace gardens to create extended chaharbaghs that could be used as royal encampments.

The geometrically shaped plots of the earlier Persian gardens were planted with fruit trees and with grape vines where the climate allowed, so they resembled orchards or vineyards. The Central Asians planted some plots of the chaharbaghs with ground cover, often clover, so they could spread their tents and awnings in the open areas for feasting.

The watercourse remained the most dominant feature in the design, though the use of water was also increased. Of ancient nature-worshipping stock, the Central Asians seemed to delight in rushing water. The play of water seems to have become more active in their gardens; from narrow channels and the large sheets of water which continued to be built from the Sassanian epoch, were added small bubbling waterfalls and gurgling fountains.

This change to active use of gardens is associated with the Ilkhans by Ralph Pinder-Wilson who studied Persian literature for a precise description of a garden. In the following passage, Dr. Pinder-Wilson describes the garden of the Golden Horde laid out in 1302 by the Ilkhans near Tabriz in northwestern Iran: "Preparations for the festivities had been begun three years previously by a large team of skilled craftsmen and engineers. A square area had been enclosed by a wall 'in order to provide a pleasant and agreeable meadow for the sojourn of the emperor.' Tanks and cisterns were installed to feed rivers and streams [watercourses]. Avenues were planted round the edge with willows to provide a passage for the populace who had to be confined to the periphery of the walled enclosure, the central area being reserved for the Golden Pavilion and the Golden Throne and the surrounding towers, baths and lofty buildings.

"This type of garden was evidently developed by the Mongols for a purpose peculiar to their own traditions and usages. The assumption of royal power required a garden setting for the nomadic encampment, and the existing Persian bagh was adapted to the requirements of the Ilkhans."[4]

The use of chaharbaghs as royal encampments was firmly established by Timur (Tamerlane, 1336–1404) in the splendid capital he built at Samarkand after his conquest of Persia. In the following century, his descendants ruled Persia and established the Mughal Dynasty in India. The ruthless Timur's name has, ironically, become synonymous with one of the most splendid periods in Persian history through his descendants, who were among the most cultivated of rulers. His son and successor, Shah Rukh, ruled in Herat for forty-three years, and presided over the most interesting court of the Timurids until his death in 1447.

Shah Rukh's biographer, Abdul Ruzzak, has left a description of a celebration which illustrates the active Timurid use of gardens: "In the royal garden were erected tents which had from 80 to 100 poles, scarlet pavilions, and tents made of silk. In these tents were thrones of gold and silver, encircled by garlands of rubies and pearls. From the carpets issued vapours of amber, whilst the durbar tent was perfumed with the soothing odor of musk . . . . Singers sang to melodious tunes the songs formerly heard at the court of the Sassanians. Skillful musicians touching deftly the lute and lyre ravished the reason of the listeners. The diversions were prolonged for many days without interruption."[5]

Shah Rukh's glittering fifteenth-century court at Herat became the center of science and art and learned men flocked there, but the Timurids' main cultural interest was in producing beautiful books. The most gifted miniaturists, paper makers, binders, and calligraphers were brought to Herat; a Library and Academy were established to assemble a great collection. This interest in manuscripts was shared by the princely Timurids who, in the next century, established the Mughal Dynasty in India. Figures appeared in paintings in these Muslim courts, though not in decoration, and the paintings became more representational. Details of garden architecture, the pavilions, walls, gates, and terrace pools, are more accurate portrayals of royal structures.

The glowing faience tile of Herat was decorated in intricate, sometimes plaited, foliated script and the *Musalla*, or complex of religious buildings and tombs, was considered the loveliest group of domes and minarets with the finest tilework in all of Asia. It stood until 1885 when the Amir, fearing a Russian attack which never materialized, razed the buildings to deny the enemy cover. Of the grove of twenty minarets, nine remained standing. Earthquakes and neglect have since claimed or weakened these. This was the fate of most Timurid architecture; a few mosques and tombs remain but no palaces have survived. What withstood the ravages of man was shaken down by tremors. A patch of garden remains behind one minaret; sadly neglected, it shows no trace of its Timurid ancestry.

The twelfth-century writer Samarqandi described the festival of the autumnal equinox in Herat, a celebration continued by the Timurids. The basil, rocket, and feverfew were in bloom, and the raisins had been stoned, dried on lines, and packed in storerooms. The valley floor was carpeted with orchards and vineyards with palaces: "each one was like highest paradise, having before it a garden or pleasure ground with a northern aspect." Describing a bountiful harvest of the exceptionally sweet grapes he wrote: "For in the district of Herat one hundred

Nymphs playing in a pool at a garden pavilion. Herat school, *ca.* 1426. (Courtesy of The Metropolitan Museum of Art, Gift of Alexander Smith Cochran)

and twenty different varieties of the grape occur, each sweeter and more delicious than the other; and amongst them are in particular two kinds which are not to be found in any other region of the inhabited world, one called Parniyan and the other Kalanjari, thin-skinned, small-stoned, and luscious, so that you would say they contained no earthly elements."[6]

51

Though there were dozens of royal gardens in the valley of Herat, only two remain, but in greatly altered condition. In 1428, Shah Rukh built a garden at Gazar Gar, the shrine of an eleventh-century Sufi saint to whom he was particularly devoted. A legend claims that this saint inspired a sixteenth-century work on gardening by appearing in a dream and instructing the author of the work.[7] Gazar Gar, though now shabby, is still a favorite spot of Heratis for family picnics.

There is a bittersweet quality to the pleasure of seeking out ruins; the contrast of past magnificence and present squalor can be startling. This feeling was conveyed by Robert Byron in 1933 when he visited the garden built by the last Timurid ruler of Herat, Husain Baiqara (1469–1506): "On the way home the landau stopped at Takht-i Safar, the Traveller's Throne, a terraced garden all in ruins whose natural melancholy was increased by the close of an autumn afternoon and the first whistle of the night wind. From the empty tank at the top, a line of pools and watercourses descends from terrace to terrace. This pleasance of Hussein Baikara was built by forced labour; for when his subjects over-stepped even his broad limits of the morally permissible, they had to help with the Sultan's garden instead of going to prison. Up till the last century there was a pavilion there, and the water was still running."[8]

While the Timurids ruled in splendor in the east, the west of Persia came under the control of the tribe of "White Sheep Turkomans" who ruled from Tabriz. Because of its proximity to Europe, Tabriz was a thriving trade center with a colony of Venetian and Genoese merchants. When it was under Ilkhan rule in the thirteenth century, Marco Polo, who had a keen commercial eye, had found that: "It is a city where good profits are made by travelling merchants. The inhabitants are a mixed lot and good for very little."[9] He added, "The city is entirely surrounded by attractive orchards, full of excellent fruit."

In an unusual gesture, the White Sheep leader, Uzan Hasan (1466–1477), attempted an alliance with Venice and entertained the ambassador, Josafa Barbaro. Barbaro later published a journal which included a description of the royal palace outside of Tabriz. The *Hasht Bihesht*, or Eight Paradises, was a spacious, two-story octagonal pavilion filled with the "most beautiful carpets." It was set in the center of a Pairidaeza with pools and broad walks. There were plantations of trees and a fine avenue of trees from the palace to the large entrance portal. Outside the gate a brick-paved *maidan*, or public square, was bordered with poplars and marble benches.

Inspired by the Eight Paradises of the Koran, palaces and gardens were often named Hasht Bihesht. The symbolism was carried through to the eight terraces or *parterres* within the chaharbaghs. The octagon was a common form for the design of pools, pavilions, and platforms. None of the orchards, gardens, or palaces of Tabriz's rich and elegant past survived for long. The city was rent and its tiled buildings leveled by several major earthquakes; what nature spared has been destroyed by war.

The brief rule of the White Sheep Turkoman ended with the start of the sixteenth century when they were overthrown by the youthful Safavid, Ismail. Persia welcomed its first native ruler in almost nine hundred years.

FIVE

The Safavids: Splendor

The Safavid rulers descended from a long line of respected holy men who had established themselves as political leaders near Ardabil in northwestern Persia. In 1501 after the Safavid Ismail, succeeded to his tribal leadership, he captured Tabriz, the capital city of the White Sheep Turkoman, and claimed the title of Shah as ruler of Persia. Within several years, he subdued his opponents in the provinces and established central rule.

Ismail, a zealous warrior and charismatic figure who made Shiism the state religion, was revered as a saint by the people who united behind him. He was intolerant of other religions; during his rule many of the Zoroastrians remaining in Persia emigrated to India.

The powerful Ottomans to the west and the Uzbeks in the east were rigidly Sunni, that is, orthodox Muslim. As a religious Shiite, Ismail regarded his campaigns against them as holy wars.

His bravery was legendary; it was said of him that "He is brave as a gamecock and stronger than any of his lords." In 1510 an incident took place which demonstrated not only his bravery but his proud character. The Uzbeks had gained control of almost all of Central Asia and continually raided the eastern cities of Persia. Ismail sent their leader, Shaibani Khan, gifts and a cautionary letter which included the following passage:

> Plant the tree of friendship for its fruit will be the desire of your heart;
> Root up the sapling of enmity, which produces countless griefs.

Shaibani's response was a rude letter accompanied by the insulting gifts of a begging bowl and a staff. Enraged, Ismail sent Shaibani a spinning wheel and spindle and the challenge to fight him and die or sit in a corner and spin. Ismail then marched on Shaibani, defeated him and destroyed him.[1]

Ismail's army of tribal bowmen, successful against the Uzbeks, was no match for the famous Janissaries of the Ottoman Turks with their muskets and artillery.[2] In a fierce campaign against the Turks, Ismail fought valiantly and risked capture, but his losses were great and his troops were routed. Legend has it that Ismail never smiled again and died when he was 38, broken by this defeat. To his people, however, he was a hero and his passing was mourned.

The second Safavid, Tahmasp (1514-1576), was a mere boy of ten with an interest in painting and was already a good calligrapher when he became Shah in 1524. Sometime after 1550, the first official contact was made between England and the closed court of Persia. The adventurer, Anthony Jenkinson, was received by Tahmasp to whom he presented letters from Queen Elizabeth. A "nonbeliever," he infuriated the Shah and barely escaped death.[3]

During Tahmasp's reign, some of the most beautiful, illuminated manuscripts in Persian literature were produced, but he became increasingly religious and in a fever of orthodoxy banned the artists from his court. The painters were forced to seek other patrons; some of the most gifted fled to the Mughal court in India, and thus began the school of Mughal miniature painting.

Tahmasp's long regime was marked by continuous hostility with his neighbors; he maintained his eastern borders, but the Ottoman Turks nibbled away at his western territories. Though weakened by a long period of anarchy following Tahmasp's death in 1576, the Safavid dynasty managed to continue though with increasingly shaky control.

Under Abbas (1587-1629), however, there came a dramatic change in Persia. Justly called the Great, Abbas secured Persia's borders, and restored its political stability, national pride, and the reputation of Persia as a power. During his long reign, Abbas undertook vast public works projects that may be seen by the traveler in Iran today: bridges, roads, shrines, mosques, and caravanserais. Abbas also finally parted the silken curtain that screened Persia and welcomed emissaries from European courts and expanded trade. All of these were great achievements but were eclipsed by his transformation of provincial Isfahan into the world-famous seventeenth-century capital—the most beautiful city of its time.

Known as Anshan when it appeared on Babylonian cuneiform tablets, Isfahan is one of the oldest continuously settled cities on the Iranian plateau. Long before Shah Abbas moved his capital there, it was blessed with the most superb mosque in Persia and one of the great buildings of the world—the Friday mosque. Begun in the eighth century, the Friday Mosque was rebuilt in the ninth, suffered a destructive fire in the twelfth, and underwent restoration and additions until the eighteenth century. Today it is sensitively and lovingly tended. Unlike most buildings in Isfahan, the Friday Mosque does not depend on color for ecstatic effect—the great surfaces are not covered in tile. A more primal religious awareness is evoked by its vast spaces and sober brickwork.

At 5,300 feet, almost completely ringed by rugged mountains, Isfahan has an agreeable climate, a pleasant setting, and the only major river on the plateau. Approaching the city, the fertile plain is broken by scattered amber villages and curious fat, round towers. At one time, there were hundreds of these pigeon towers; a large one could house thousands of birds. The droppings collected in the center wells were used for fertilizer on the famous Isfahan melon beds.

In the seventeenth century, the waters of the Zaindeh Rud were high in spring, but the river was reduced to a trickle by autumn, and the Isfahanis used underground cisterns for water storage. Abbas's garden city on the northern bank required a new intricate irrigation system, which was, in effect, terraced. Each stone-lined canal ran from the river to the northeast and watered the land

Isfahan. Courtyard of Madrassa Madar-i Shah
with seventeenth-century maddi running
through it.

on its south side. Six canals, called *Maddi,* remain; one Maddi still runs through
the courtyard of the Safavid Madrassa Mader-i Shah, which is beautifully restored
and retains a stately atmosphere.

Anxious to complete his new capital, Abbas drove his workmen, and sometimes he apparently sacrificed structural soundness for speed. Of his original
plan, the largest and most important surviving feature is the vast twenty-acre
maidan. Almost 1,700 feet long and 550 feet wide, enclosed in a two-story arcade,
it was the site of assemblies and favorite royal entertainments—punishments,
parades, and polo; the marble goal posts stand there today. To the north of the
maidan lay the large, covered main bazaar which was entered through a tall iwan
centered in the arcade; at the opposite end of the maidan was the Masjid-i Shah.
The dome of this tiled mosque is like the heavenly garden; the floral arabesques
against the background of varying blues which could be the heavens or water.
To the west of the mosque a palace, the Ali Qapu, served as the king's
grandstand overlooking the maidan and as the entrance to the royal enclosure.
During recent restoration of the Ali-Qapu palace, lead pipes were discovered in
the walls, and, on the second story, is a decorative basin lined with lead. Lead
pipes have been found at other royal sites dating from this era. Abbas did not
construct one sizable palace; instead he built a series of contiguous gardens,
each with a palace or large pavilion which served a different function. In the
Chehel Sutan or hall of forty columns, he received many foreign visitors; in other

gardens there were banqueting pavilions, the women's pavilions, and the king's private pavilion. Originally these royal gardens overlooked the tree-lined Chahar Bagh Avenue to the west.

The axis of Abbas's geometric plan for Isfahan was the innovative Chahar Bagh Avenue. Most gardens were square or rectangular; the Chahar Bagh Avenue was a ribbon of garden which ran a mile to the river. It has been said that the name derived from the fact that it cut through four vineyards to reach the river.[4] Down the center ran a stone watercourse, faced in onyx, carrying water through a series of square or octagonal pools on several levels. This main channel was intersected by the irrigation canals and planted with eight rows of chenars, the oriental plane, and poplars. Paved paths flanked the watercourse, and rose hedges and flower beds stretched beneath the trees to the defining walls. Courtiers and merchants built ornately painted and gilded palaces set in square chaharbaghs along the avenue and the riverbanks.

On a tour of the Near East almost two hundred years later, the artist, Sir Robert Ker Porter, was moved by the Chahar Bagh Avenue: "We passed through the most charming parts of the Chahar Bagh; taking our course along its alleys of unequalled plane trees, stretching their broad canopies over our heads, their shade being rendered yet more delightful by the canals, reservoirs, fountains, which cooled the air, and reflected the flickering light through their branches. Thickets of roses and jessamine, with clustering parterres of poppies, and other flowers embanked the ground; while the deep-green shadows from the trees, the perfume, the freshness, the soft gurgling of the waters, and the gentle rustle of the breeze, combining with the pale golden rays of the declining sun, altogether formed an evening scene, as tranquilizing as it was beautiful."[5]

Today, Isfahan is a bustling modern city, and the Chahar Bagh Avenue has

Isfahan. Shah Abbas's Chehel Sutan, or hall of forty columns, reflected in large rectangular pool.

been narrowed to a commercial strip lined with shops, crowded with busy shoppers, and noisy with traffic; a mall covers the old watercourse.

At the river the Chahar Bagh met the Pul Ali Varden Khan, an unusual bridge built on two levels with arcaded walkways. On the southern bank of the river, gardens extended in both directions. In 1659 an aqueduct, four meters wide, was built to carry water from the canals on the northern side across to the continuing royal gardens. It is now a footbridge across the Zaindeh Rud. Three miles beyond these southern gardens, yet linked to the city by a continuation of the Chahar Bagh Avenue, Shah Abbas built a Pairidaeza, the Hazar Jarib. It was described by the Huguenot jeweler, Sir John Chardin, who visited in 1665, as a mile square and having twelve terraces and fountains with lead pipes.[6]

Seventy years after Chardin's visit, Shah Sultan Husain laid out Farahabad, a garden reported to be even larger than Abbas's Pairidaeza, which it adjoined. It is said that Husain was so fond of this garden he offered to surrender the city of Isfahan to the invading Afghans if they would leave him in peace in Farahabad. The Afghans took both the city and the garden and burned Husain's garden palace to the ground.

Of the dozens of palaces which once lined the Chahar Bagh Avenue and the river's banks, only one remains: the *Hasht Bihesht* or Eighth Paradise. It was in this romantic palace situated in the center of the Garden of the Nightingale that Chardin was lodged. Carefully restored, exquisitely and intricately painted, the Hasht Bihesht seems hardly more substantial than the colorful embroidered tents of the old Timurid encampments.

Within the brick and stucco walls of the Chehel Sutan Palace grounds where Abbas received official visitors, the paths and plots have been changed, but the enclosure is the original size and the proportions of palace, pool, and garden are harmoniously balanced. The airy, painted palace seems to combine older Persian traditions. The use of exceedingly tall decorative columns and the stone lions, here used as fountains, recalls Achaemenid details; the extended, reflecting pool, the Sassanian palace settings.[7]

The Safavid kings had a passionate fondness for great carpets and took the kind of personal interest in carpet weaving that previous monarchs had in manuscripts and painting.

In the Safavid workshops, the theme of the garden continued to be the main decorative inspiration for Persian carpet designs just as floral motifs continued to pervade all Persian art. Widely used in Persia, carpets were traditionally the main furnishings of homes and palaces; aside from cushions, there was very little other furniture. They were spread outside as well: in gardens for entertainments, on the ground for festivals. The distinctive carpets of Shah Abbas's era were the so-called vase carpets. These had a bold floral design isolated on a field of solid color in the center. The lotus in splendid, imaginative, multiple interpretations was common. On some carpets, the center design was the outline of a vine leaf enclosing a pool bordered with flowers. It is interesting that the ancient Persian symbols of fertility and water appear in these carpets.

However cosmopolitan his capital had become,[8] the energetic Abbas was not content to remain there; he loved the Caspian Coast and built a series of terraced, hillside chaharbaghs overlooking the sea. To make the journey less hazardous

Kashan. Bagh-i Fin. Central
watercourse with fountains;
pebble-paved walks lead to
central pavilion.

and more comfortable for his ladies, he constructed a series of caravanserais
and royal lodges every twelve miles or so—the equivalence of a day's journey—
along the route across the desert and through the mountains. Skirting the
western edge of the great salt desert running northeast from Kashan, Abbas built
a road—the *Sang Farsh*, or stone carpet—of rough stone blocks about a foot
square.

A few miles southwest of the dusty old desert city of Kashan at the site of an
ancient spring on the first slopes of the mountains, Abbas built the Garden of
Fin in 1590. It is the oldest garden in good condition to be seen in Iran today. It
is believed that another Safavid garden existed nearby, and that a polo ground
extended between the two. Polo, played in Persia for many centuries, was the
favorite sport of the active Abbas. Just beyond this supposed polo ground,
between the Garden of Fin and the city of Kashan, rise the archaeological
mounds of Siyalk, a farming settlement of the fifth millennium B.C.[9]

Within the garden, the sound of rushing water fills the cool air beneath dense
rows of 390-year-old cypress trees towering above the silver water in the channels.
The source of the water is a qanat and a powerful spring outside the high,
protective mud walls at the rear of the garden. A domed pavilion and large
octagonal pool were built over the spring in the nineteenth century. Such a
spring is a precious local resource, and its use is carefully monitored. The
translucent water is divided into four channels: one feeds the garden, the others
water the neighboring fields and farms. Part of the run-off from the garden flows
into a flour mill nearby. The share of water allowed the garden is five-elevenths of
the output which runs at 600 litres a second and is constant year round. The
temperature of the water in the pool varies only a few degrees throughout the
year. When the air is cold, the water seems warm under the winter sun; in

summer heat, there is a temptation to join the "jube fish" swimming in and out of the cress growing up through the natural rocky bottom.

Beneath the rear wall and just inside the garden, water bubbles up forcefully, like a spring, through a large opening in the center of a square pool. Nearby is a second pool which was originally lined with eight-by-eight-inch square blue tiles each of which had a foliated opening in the center. The tiles are gone now, but the bottom of the shallow pool is perforated by three-inch holes for the water to enter. From these pools, the water pours into the stone watercourses which divide the garden. The terracing throughout Fin is rather shallow, averaging eighteen inches, with small cascades at each change in level. The hundreds of fountains lining the channels, careful reproductions of the originals, are typical of fountains in old gardens. They were quite simple, made of either carved stone or, as in Fin, of ceramic with a single jet and without a nozzle. The fountains were gravity-fed by a simple forcing system. A second channel ran beneath the visible canal decorated with fountains. This lower channel could be blocked at the end of each terrace forcing the water up through the fountain.

The walks of the chaharbagh, which flank the watercourses, are paved with large pebbles set in mud in a triangular pattern. The old *humman*, or bath, is in good condition. In the mid-nineteenth century, it was the scene of a murder which had consequences felt throughout Persia as related in the following legend. The incorruptible vizier, Mirza Taqi Khan, had instituted reforms which angered members of the ruling family and the court, and the Shah was encouraged by his jealous mother to murder the learned and saintly vizier. Hired assassins killed

Kashan. Bagh-i Fin. Waterchute flanked by steps. This is typical of the change in level between the shallow terraces throughout garden.

59

Mirza Taqi Khan as he enjoyed the baths in the Bagh-i Fin. The main pavilion, which dates from a later period, is being restored. The Bagh-i Fin is an elegant and captivating garden, where it is not difficult to imagine the color and pageantry of the Safavid court.

In 1626, the ambassador of Charles I, Sir Dodmore Cotton, the first official envoy from England, arrived in Isfahan after a long and arduous journey from London. He learned to his dismay that he must continue on to the Caspian Coast where Abbas wished to receive him. The ambassador was accompanied on his trade mission by a youthful and lively observer, Sir Thomas Herbert. The additional 400-mile trip took them through the "valley of the angel of death," so-called because of legends of ghouls and monsters, across the salt desert and over almost impassable mountains. Sir Thomas described the rigors of almost a month, "travelling all the night and reposing (I cannot say sleeping, the Gnats so troubled us) all the day.

"We had guides and a Convoy to direct us, the Starres were theirs, without whose ayme there is no certaintie. The Sunne is so firey and makes the Sands so scalding on the day time, that it then prohibits Pilgrimages." [10]

More than 260 years later, another English traveler in Persia, Lord Curzon, then a youthful journalist, described a night meeting with a caravan. The ghostly midnight passages were unchanged: "Out of the black darkness is heard the distant boom of a heavy bell. Mournfully, and with perfect regularity of iteration, it sounds, gradually swelling nearer and louder, and perhaps mingling with the tones of smaller bells, signalling the rearguard of the same caravan. The big bell is the insignia and alarum of the leading camel alone. But nearer and louder as the sound becomes, not another sound, and not a visible object, appears to accompany it. Suddenly, and without the slightest warning, there looms out of the darkness, like the apparition of a phantom ship, the form of the captain of the caravan. His spongy tread sounds softly on the smooth sand, and, like a great string of linked ghouls, the silent procession stalks by and is swallowed up in the night." [11]

Sudden violent hot winds can sweep across the desert and suffocate travelers with stinging clouds of sand. The great bactrian camels have saved many caravans by their ability to sense the coming onslaught. [12]

Lord Curzon's predecessor, Sir Thomas, found the Dasht-i Kavir, or great salt desert, a misery as "nothing but salt (not unlike pure snow) where note that the whole wilderness is so deepe and boggie, that Horse, Cammell, or Elephant, if they goe from the Causey are plunged and buried in the Salt and Bogge." [13]

What a lift to the exhausted spirits of such battered travelers must have been the dark pinnacles of the cypress trees above the sheltering walls of a Persian garden. After days of agony and nights of terror, Sir Thomas and his party reached such a paradise—one of Shah Abbas's royal gardens along their sandy route to the Caspian Coast:

"Tawgehawt, a House and Garden of the Kings, giving place to few in Parthia.... The Garden is North from the House yethjoyning to it, it has six severall discents, each part giving eightie paces, and seventie broad, this watered by a cleare rivolet (tho little) by whose vertue it abounds in Damaske Roses and other flowers, plentie of broad spreading Chenar trees (which is like our Beech) with Pomegranats, Peaches, Apricockes, Plummes, Apples, Peares, Chestnuts

Taj-i abad. Ruins of the watercourse and pavilion described by Sir Thomas Herbert.

and Cherries. It has Ecchoes, naturall Grottoes and Labyrinths, made by art and nature. It enjoyes a Hot-house well built and paved with white Marble, and these are the rarer, because they are seated and walled about, in a large even Plaine, rich in nothing but Salt and Sand." [14]

Known today as Taj-Abad, the chaharbagh visited by Sir Thomas can be found by tracing the old caravan route. A remarkable number of Safavid hunting lodges and gardens can still be identified on the old route north from Isfahan. Some are ruins, some have been converted to other purposes and some, like Taj-Abad, are now privately owned and farmed. At Taj-Abad almost three of the original seven terraces remain. A garden that faces south, it has an ideal location and view with snow-capped mountains not too distant to the north and an open plain sloping gently away from it. A qanat line runs from the mountains and the water flows cold, clear and quickly in the jubes through the small village built against the wall of the garden. The villagers farm the land and store their grain in the ruins of Shah Abbas's pavilion. The cypress and chenar trees are gone, and poplars now outline the remaining terraces. Ancient foot-thick grape vines and old rose bushes border the attractive, irregularly paved stone paths. The narrow stone watercourse is empty, and only three water chutes remain. They are carved in one of the most familiar scalloped patterns; in Persia they call it pigeon breast, in India, where the water-chute is called a *chaddar,* the pattern is called fish scales.

Once over the exhausting heights and through the tortuous rocky defiles of the Elbruz Range, the English travelers found themselves in a world far removed

61

Abbasabad. Ruins of royal hunting lodge in large terraced garden. Oasis-like character of the gardens at the edge of the salt desert is dramatically demonstrated here.

from the monotonous stone ridges and tawny desert of the plateau. Here the dangers bordering Abbas's northern Sang Farsh were not deadly salt flats, but mosquito- and reptile-infested swamps.

The northern slopes of the Elbruz seen by the seventeenth-century travelers were covered with familiar European trees growing in unfamiliar jungle richness and entwined by vines. The thick undergrowth harbored tigers, leopards, jackals, bears, boar, and deer. The vegetation was so dense that these travelers were often startled by the sudden emergence of villages; Shah Abbas had uprooted thousands of Christian families from his Turkish border and placed them in settlements he expanded along the Caspian Coast.[15] Chardin found the "air is so unwholsom" that by 1630 the "30,000 Christian families were reduced to 400" probably by malaria or "the fluxe" which claimed the life of the exhausted Sir Dodmore Cotton in 1627.

As they had before, the travelers sought refuge in gardens. If the enclosing walls of a Pairidaeza on the plateau had been a relief from the broad barren desert, here the garden walls offered protection from the dense tropical vegetation. In his northern gardens, Abbas took advantage of the steep slope of the Elbruz and the abundance of water to build terraced, hillside gardens with rushing water cascading from level to level. At Ashraf, a complex of five contiguous gardens, his own garden, the Bagh-i Shah, consisted of ten terraces on the mountain slope.

Sir Thomas climbed the mountain beyond Ashraf and enjoyed a visit to the hot sulphur baths there. The sulphur springs in the mountains probably explain the comments by all visitors to Ashraf on the "especially salubrious" nature of the water in the gardens.

The cultural borrowing which existed in prehistory between the plateau and the Indus valley never ceased, and at Ashraf we see the influence of the gardens of Mughal India, particularly in the pavilion spanning the watercourse. The plan of Ashraf is not as refined as the Mughal gardens of Kashmir; the watercourses are narrower and lack the fountains. The large pools, called *dariacheh*, or little sea, actually stone-edged ponds, which Abbas seems to have favored, seem out of proportion to the terraces.

Ashraf was a few miles above Astrabad Bay, and Abbas must have had a splendid view of the varied waterfowl which nested in the reeds and islands of the Bay. Coots, snipes, ducks, cormorants, geese, cranes, swans, must surely have entertained him with their aerobatics. Abbas used Bagh-i Shah for diversion; as described by Sir Thomas Herbert and other guests, the entertainments in the garden pavilions were more like orgies than royal banquets.

An admirable ruler, Abbas was not an attractive person. He is described as small, wiry, energetic, very quick and clever, but deeply suspicious and of a

Detail of waterchute in shell, or pigeon breast, pattern.

mercurial disposition. His cruelty was so excessive that his own sons did not escape torture. Court life was luxurious—even decadent—and, reflecting the taste of the feared Shah, there was a marked taste for the sensuous and erotic.

Scarcely two days' march, only twenty-six miles from Ashraf, Abbas built a very similar group of chaharbaghs at Farahbad. It was here he died in 1628, in the forty-third year of his reign. Chardin, who spent ten years traveling in Persia, later reflected that "When Shah Abbas died Persia ceased to live."

Following his death the cycle of Persian history was repeated; periods of domestic decay, foreign domination, and the emergence of independent Persian rule. There were long periods when gardens were not built or maintained, and the mud walls crumbled. The gardens became tangled thickets of weeds and the trees were cut by people needing firewood.

One of the few imaginative gardens constructed later was the Bagh-i Takht or Garden of the Throne, built in Shiraz in 1789. Set on a hillside with seven steep, shallow terraces, it overlooked a large rectangular pool. An unusual feature was the series of rooms and stairways built into the hillside under each terrace. Today only two pavilions remain, and the watercourse and pool are gone. On the top level, a bit of caved-in earth exposes a flight of stairs and one of the deep rooms inside the hill. The construction was of heavy timbers and the common 7½-by-7½-by-2-inch fired brick.

Sir Thomas Herbert thought Shiraz grapes the best in Asia and the wine "like the French but better tasted." He credited the binding quality of Shiraz wine with saving his life. Shiraz is still famous for its wine and gardens. The city has several well-known gardens; the most authentic is the recently restored courtyard

Yazd. Detail of a pool within garden.

chaharbagh within the handsome but forbidding brick walls of the Citadel.

Though it bears a much older name, the Bagh-i Eram was rebuilt and planted in the nineteenth century with rows of cypresses and umbrella pines which are now mature and stately. There has been a garden at the site of the Dilgusha since 1737. It is a very large orange grove bordered by cypress trees and the sour orange which has adapted to temperatures which lower to fifteen degrees in the winter. Generally in Shiraz, foreign influence dominates in the flower beds and general maintenance is actually creeping modernization.

It is difficult to find an old, exclusively Persian garden in Iran today. However, some remain in remote old cities like Yazd, and their character and atmosphere make them well worth the search. Along with mechanized wells, traditional methods of water collection and distribution are still in use in the interesting isolated desert city of Yazd. There is no oasis there and the land does not look as if it could support any life at all. Perhaps the particularly inhospitable aspect of the desert protected Yazd from Mongol invasions. Or perhaps, as the Yazdis believe, the city escaped sacking because it was never a capital. The present city is 1,200 years old and is built on the site of an even older settlement.

Scarcity of water is an historic problem for Yazd, for the average annual rainfall there is two centimeters. Until recently, water came from dug wells called *chehel zar* or forty meters, referring to the former average depth to the subterranean water level. With the city's growth and increased needs, the drilled wells are now more than three times that depth. Qanat lines from a mountain affectionately referred to as "the sleeping lion" still supply most outlying areas.

One can still find in Yazd a man chosen to supervise water distribution in the

Yazd Bad-gir above the gatehouse; yak chal in background.

traditional manner. From a central source—a reservoir or qanat—water flows through an irrigation canal to each field for a specific length of time. The flow is controlled by a simple, metal barrage. A brass bowl with a one-centimeter hole in the bottom is the measurement; it takes one hour for the bowl to empty.

Yazd is one of the hottest spots on the plateau; in summer, the temperature can average 44 degrees Centigrade. Rows of trees are necessary along roads and the edge of the city to hold the soil and serve as windbreaks against the blowing desert sands. As precious water would be lost under the searing sun, open jubes are not used to water trees. Following an old local custom, an earthenware jar is buried between rows of trees with only its neck above ground. When filled with water, the porous jar sweats and thus nourishes the roots.

A few miles outside the city is an extensive garden which the same family has owned and lived in for over two centuries. Continuing older traditions, this private garden provides an accurate picture of eighteenth-century gardens.

A qanat line runs seventy kilometers from the south; some water is used for the enclosed garden and a larger share irrigates the surrounding farmland. The garden—24,000 square meters—has always been famous for its pomegranates which still grow there along with rows of cherry trees. One turkey and a flock of chickens scratch the earth beneath the fruit trees.

A two-story pavilion, the family's residence, sits on a high platform in the center of the garden. A cruciform pool, thirty-six feet in diameter, with a low fountain bubbling up in the center, lies on the south side of the pavilion. The overflow from this pool runs into the jubes irrigating the plots of fruit trees. On the northern side, a quiet, long, key-hole-shaped pool reflects the brilliant sky. Throughout the garden the pebble-paved walks are bordered by plane trees.

The roof of the large gatehouse is a series of small domes and has the appearance of a small village. This building houses the stables, storerooms, carriage house, and humman. Above it towers a *bad-gir* or wind tower—a structure common in cities edging the great desert—which catches any breeze and funnels it to the summer livingroom beneath the main pavilion. Opposite the entrance gate is the *ab ambir*, an underground water reservoir covered by a deep half-dome. Nearby stands the abstract form, the *yak chal*, a tall curving wall which shadows a shallow pool of water in winter causing it to freeze; the ice is cut and stored underground for summer use.

This extensive self-sufficient complex is referred to as a garden, but it is obviously much more. The Persians so love their gardens that they have always applied the word to their country houses. The peaceful but purposeful routine of life within these walls has probably changed very little since they were first built.

Within Yazd's city walls, Doulat-a Bagh, a formal Safavid garden built about 1712 as a residence for the governor, is under restoration by the government of Iran. The research has been extensive, and the gardens and buildings are being faithfully reconstructed.

Doulat-a Bagh covers about twenty-seven acres and is actually two gardens: a private garden for the official family, and a ceremonial garden. They are separated by high walls and the winter pavilion. The governor dealt with the severe climatic changes by moving with the seasons. In the cold winter months, he lived in the winter pavilion which was built with a southern exposure to catch all possible sunlight. Under the torrid sun of summer, he moved to the dark summer pavilion which faced the north and was cooled by five interior pools with trickling fountains and breezes funneled through the tall bad-gir.

Water is so precious in Yazd that there is no open watercourse, and the central axis between the two buildings is planted with clover. Avenues of tall dark trees line the broad paths flanking the clover bed. The side plots are planted with pomegranate and cherry trees with furrows between them. Plots of grape vines flank the summer pavilion.

The garden was originally irrigated by a share of water from several qanats running from the south, but it now has its own drilled well. All the pools and fountains in Yazd are lined with a mixture of clay, ash, and lime called *sarvage* which makes a hard, watertight surface. Sarvage is the traditional material also used in Kerman, 200 miles to the southeast, where the fountains are modeled of it in a simple style with a single jet.

The walls enclosing the private garden of Doulat-a Bagh housed the harem and kitchen. The staff lived in the gate house. The walls were unusual, with walkways along the top, and punctuated by squat watchtowers, decorated with brickwork. There were quarters for the governor's guards and a large guest house built into the walls of the official garden.

In Iran today, gardeners are called *bagh ban* which means guardian of the garden. Perpetuating the ancient traditions, the bagh ban of Yazd plant fruit trees in the symmetrical groves enjoyed by Cyrus the Younger in his pairidaeza in 401 B.C.

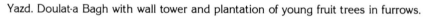

Yazd. Doulat-a Bagh with wall tower and plantation of young fruit trees in furrows.

CONCLUSION

Since the age of Cyrus, invaders, adventurers and merchants who penetrated the mountains ringing the plateau were enchanted by the gardens they found there. The Greeks and Romans were merely the first to carry the tradition away with them.

It was many centuries before the Europeans developed landscape traditions that were distinctly their own. Then, European visitors to Persia began to be critical of some of the old garden practices which they found monotonous, such as the rigidly geometric garden layout and the invariable use of fruit trees.

In the nineteenth century, Lord Curzon, in describing a Persian garden, revealed a longing for the broad view across an English lawn: "They are planted down the sides of long alleys, admitting of no view but a vista, the surrounding plots being a jungle of bushes and shrubs. Water courses along in channels or is conducted into tanks. Sometimes these gardens rise in terraces to a pavilion at the summit, whose reflection in the pool below is regarded as a triumph of landscape gardening. There are no neat walks, or shaped flower beds, or stretches of sward. All is tangled and untrimmed. Such beauty as arises from shade and the purling of water is all that the Persian requires." [16]

Lord Curzon, generally so sensitive to Persian culture, in his nostalgic mood had momentarily forgotten that the very features he criticized were what made the garden a peaceful sanctuary for the Persian. Where the sky is truly infinite, and the desert nearly so till broken by the scarped rock of barren mountain ranges, what a relief and pleasure is a narrow vista defined by densely planted trees. The Persian not only conquered a hostile environment by the geometric layout of his verdant garden and its use of shimmering water, but equally important he saw in it the promise and abundance of Paradise.

CENTRAL ASIA

SIX

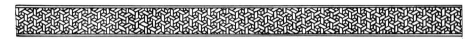

Timur

The River Oxus, now called the Amu Darya, is a natural boundary between the seemingly endless steppes of Central Asia, and eastern Persia and, to the south, what is now Afghanistan. However, throughout history the river never deterred mounted invaders led by ambitious world conquerors. Transoxiana was annexed to the Achaemenid Empire by Darius I in the fifth century B.C. and designated as the satrapy of Sughuda. It was called Sogdiana by the Greeks who united it with Bactria. The coveted source of lapis lazuli and carnelian, Transoxiana was taken by the Scythians in the second century B.C., and later it became a major province of the Parthians who had a splendid capital and vast vineyards at Nisa. The region was engulfed by the tide of Arab invaders late in the seventh century. After initial strong resistance, the settled people converted to Islam.

The customs of the invaders were absorbed into the existing primitive culture of this remote part of the world. The rituals of Siberian Shamanism which had been widely practiced in archaic times were slow to disappear and some of these beliefs remained with the superstitious Central Asians.[1] In their myths were traces of the culture of distant lands including the ancient Persians and Meso-potamians. Buddhist influence, and with it Indian culture, came later but were quite strong.

Following the swift and savage Mongol invasion in the early thirteenth century, there was strict adherence to the Mongol code and the strictures of Jenghiz Khan, including a continued dedication to the encampment rather than to settled life.[2]

Regardless of who ruled, an essentially nomadic, pastoral life persisted for centuries. This was compatible with the nature-worshipping background of the people. It was customary for the ruler to spend winters in his capital and to move with his attendants and army to well-watered pasture grounds in the spring. Here man and beast found food plentiful and regained their strength for battle. In peacetime, this migration enabled the ruler to tour his lands, choosing a different encampment each summer.

The very land of Transoxiana is legendary. In the second century B.C., Ptolemy indicated in his *Guide to Geography* that the four rivers of Paradise originated there. Given Arabic names by the medieval Arabs, the two major rivers, the Oxus and Jaxartes, were thought to be two of the four great rivers.

The population clustered around the oasis cities which prospered as long as the old caravan routes linked Europe and India with China; with the opening of the sea routes they declined. The meadows ringing these cities stretched to the horizon, gradually becoming treeless, semi-desert plains before tapering off into undulating desert. The meadows provided grazing land, and in the spring, were like gardens of wild flowers. The pasture land diminished in the summer; extremes in temperature were great—summers parched by hot desert winds were followed by severely cold winters. The yearly rainfall was capricious and varied tremendously; the area depended on irrigation from glacier-fed streams and melting snow fields in the Pamir chain.

The loess soil of the steppes is a rich, wind-blown loam which is very productive when watered. Unlike the mud bricks of Persia, bricks made of loess harden like concrete because of its calcium deposits. These bricks were the common building material of the oasis cities, and the extremely thick walls withstood the frequent, violent earthquakes very well. It is not surprising that nature cults hung on tenaciously in this land of great natural contrasts.

In the fourteenth century, this area was known as the Fourth Mongol Empire and was ruled by the Chagatai, descendants of the second son of Jenghiz Khan. The territory had been split into dozens of fiefdoms resulting in constant skirmishing among the chieftains, and there was great hostility between the nomadic Mongols and the settled Muslim population in the oasis cities. Suddenly, Timur emerged from obscurity and gained power by taking advantage of this political fragmentation. A Barlas Turk and a Muslim, Timur often misrepresented his ancestry in order to claim relationship to the Khan. [3]

By 1369, having won Samarkand, Timur began his foreign conquests. He invaded Persia in 1380, occupied Moscow in 1390, and led the bloody conquest of Delhi in 1398. He moved across Armenia, and in 1402 defeated the Ottoman Turks. His horde was said to move "like locusts over a green field."

After each victory, he would send the plunder back to Samarkand, his capital, which he intended to make the most impressive city in the world. When he first took Samarkand, it was a city still crumbling in the dust from Jenghiz Khan's raid. He rebuilt the city obsessively; enormous buildings covered with fabulously decorated tile appeared almost overnight. Some, like the Bibi Khannum Mosque, were built too quickly for their size and soon collapsed. Timur evidently took special pride in the gardens which became known throughout the world. It is one of history's quirks that such a brutal warrior was so important in the history of a great garden tradition and was the ancestor of men who attained such high artistic achievement: the Timurids of Persia and the Mughals of India.

The attraction of the Persian garden was very great for Timur for it suited his needs perfectly. Within the garden walls he could create a luxurious encampment that befitted a world conqueror and could decorate his pavilions with plunder from captive nations. He made his throne the platform above the watercourses which represented the four rivers of life; thus he symbolically ruled the four

71

quarters. He chose to live in the splendid gardens he built at Samarkand and frequently moved from one to another.

Timur built gardens in conquered lands as well. Ahmed Ibn Arabshah, an educated boy from Baghdad, was taken prisoner and brought to Samarkand. Though severely critical of Timur, he wrote that when Timur laid waste a great city he would build a palace and gardens. He also claimed that it was customary for the people of Samarkand to use Timur's gardens when he was abroad on a campaign: "the citizens, rich and poor, went to walk therein and found no retreat more wonderful or beautiful than those and no resting place more agreeable and secure; and its sweetest fruits were common to all."[4]

Timur was known as Tamerlane in the West, a corruption of Timur-i-Leng meaning Timur the Lame, from an injury he received as a youth. Apparently physically impressive in spite of this, he was exceptionally tall and broad shouldered. White-haired from youth, he wore a long beard and had "eyes like candles, without brilliance."[5] He evidently possessed a strange personal quality which inspired awe and attracted devoted followers. He was intelligent, decisive, tenacious, and fearless; he was also deceitful, ruthless, merciless, and vengeful. It was said of him "He did not love jest and falsehood; wit and sport pleased him not; truth, though troublesome to him, pleased him; he was not sad in adversity or joyful in prosperity."[6] The cult of the hero was always strong in Central Asia, and in the nineteenth century travelers still heard old Turkoman legends of Timur.

Timur caught the attention of the Christian kings of the West by defeating the Ottoman Turks who threatened Constantinople. Though Europe feared his advance, they regarded him as something of a savior for, surprisingly, he left the city of Christian relics untouched and returned to Samarkand. The legend of Timur later captured the imagination of the West when Christopher Marlowe immortalized him in *Tamburlaine the Great*. That the West hailed Timur with seeming piety and gratitude as "the Scourge of God" is ironic in the light of history.

In 1403, King Henry III of Spain sent an embassy bearing gifts on the long journey to Timur at Samarkand. The delegation was led by his chamberlain, Ruy Gonzales de Clavijo, whose famous account of the visit has survived intact. Clavijo's narrative made an impact when published and, as the only extant description of Samarkand under Timur, remains an invaluable source today.

Clavijo, accompanied by a friar and an officer of the royal guard, spent fifteen months traveling from Cadiz to Samarkand. They found Timur at seventy almost blind, too weak to mount a horse, but still in total control of his kingdom and the assembled horde camped in the meadows around Samarkand.

He received the Spaniards graciously in the *Dilkusha*, or Garden of Heart's-ease. Located about five kilometers east of Samarkand, Bagh-i Dilkusha was approached from the Turquoise Gate of the city along an avenue of white poplars. Several miles long, this avenue passed through a great meadow called the Quail Reserve. The gardens and meadows around Samarkand were usually given poetic names: World's Picture, Garden of Paradise, Meadow of the Deep Pool.[7]

The Spaniards entered the chaharbagh through a high gateway "beautifully

Zafar-nama. European envoys present the son of the Ottoman Sultan to Timur. Painted in Persia in the century following Timur's death, this portrays him in a Persian turban *Life of Timur,* 1529. (Gullistan Palace Library, Tehran)

ornamented with tile work in gold and blue." Inside they were surprised by six Indian elephants, bearing howdahs and performing tricks. Everywhere they looked silken tents and awnings gaily decorated the garden. As they passed through successive enclosures, they were received by Timurid princes seated on raised platforms. "Then coming to the presence beyond we found Timur and he was seated under what might be called a portal which same was before the entrance of a most beautiful palace that appeared in the background. He was sitting on the ground, but upon a raised dais before which there was a fountain that threw up a column of water into the air backwards, and in the basin of the fountain there were floating red apples. His Highness had taken his place on what appeared to be small mattresses stuffed thick and covered with embroidered silk cloth, and he was leaning on his elbow against some round cushions that were heaped up behind him."[8]

The ambassadors, called "Franks" by the courtiers, thought the most beautiful garden was the newly built Bagh-i Naw, or New Garden. "This orchard was surrounded by a high wall, four square, enclosing it, and at each of the four corners was a very lofty round tower, and the enclosing wall going from tower to tower was very high built, and as strong as the work of the tower. This orchard in its centre had a great palace, built on the plan of a cross, and a very large water-tank had been dug before it. This palace with its large garden was much the finest of any that we had visited hitherto, and in the ornamentation of its buildings in the gold and blue tile work far the most sumptuous."[9]

Autumn, the time of Clavijo's visit, was the driest season in this area of little annual rainfall and the loess was borne in dusty clouds along the meadows and roads. Even at royal entertainments within the gardens, Clavijo complained, "Further the dust round and about was blown up so thick that our faces and clothing became all of one colour and covered by it." Between visits to court, the Spaniards were relieved at being able to spend time quietly in the vast royal chaharbagh where they were housed some distance outside the city. Clavijo described it as "a full league round and within it is full of fruit trees of all kinds, save only limes and citron-trees which we noticed to be lacking." The winters of Transoxiana are severe and citrus trees cannot survive the frost. This chaharbagh was approached through an equally large vineyard, its walls bordered by shade trees. The garden had a central watercourse which dropped six levels as it passed through six large tanks. Paved paths raised above the planting beds were lined with shade trees, and game grazed throughout.

The variety of game in Timur's gardens was not equal to the menageries of the Sassanian kings, but the diplomatic party brought an exotic addition for his collection. The Spaniards were accompanied by an ambassador from the Sultan of Egypt who presented Timur with a giraffe. This hardy animal walked all the way from Cairo to Samarkand—three thousand miles.

In a monograph on Timurid gardens the Soviet scholar, Dr. Galina A. Pugachenkova, lists fourteen gardens in Samarkand and mentions that the Dilkusha was laid out by Timur in 1378 for his twelve-year old bride.[10] She writes that Timur was proud of his gardens and lived "like a guest" in the pavilions.

Dr. Pugachenkova included a description of excavations conducted in 1941 at the site of a luxurious humman and garden of Ulugh Beg, Timur's grandson who ruled Samarkand after his death. The site, now lost in the modern expansion of the city, was directly opposite the huge madrassa of Ulugh Beg in Registan Square in modern Samarkand. Finds included ceramic pipes for an underground water system, brick and marble paving on several levels, and unlined irrigation ditches edging the garden.

Pugachenkova concluded that the fifteenth-century gardens of Central Asia "had a strictly established plan, based on a system of geometrically structured axes (two or more) issuing from a single point, which was the owner's palace or house, and being characterized by a picturesque freedom of intimate landscapes within the confines of this specific plan, which included clumps of trees. Architecture, vegetation, and water supplement each other harmoniously, combining garden, pool, palace and pavilions into one organic whole."

According to Pugachenkova, Timur planned the gardens personally and, where possible, included existing chenar trees, removing trees only if they violated the desired symmetry. Continuous bloom is not possible in the climate of Samarkand, but Pugachenkova claims that Timur planned his garden to have blossoms as long as possible. In a "reconstruction of a plan of a standard chaharbagh of the of the Timurid epoch," she lists the most common flowers: yellow and white jasmine, marigolds, eight varieties of roses, crocus, narcissus, violets, anenomes, iris as borders along paths, including lemon iris and the white steppe variety. Among the shrubs and trees were quince, peach, sweet cherry, apricot, mulberry, plane and poplar. Peonies had a prominent place and "vintage" grapes were included. Clover was used for ground cover.

Though we can reconstruct the layout of these old gardens, it is difficult to confirm what plant material was used. By the fourteenth century there had been centuries of trading and hybridization of plants, and a gardener such as Timur would have collected a number of plants on his travels. Including some unlisted native plants, there are many possible additions to Pugachenkova's list which would provide for a longer period of color in Timur's gardens.

Clavijo's *Embassy to Tamerlane* supplements the account of the gardens' appearance with a vivid description of how they were used. September 1404 was a time of continual feasting as the court celebrated the marriage of six of Timur's grandsons. The festivities were held in various royal chaharbaghs ringing the city. Large, lavishly embroidered tents erected on the broad terraces were crowded with hundreds of family members and guests: chiefs, amirs, ministers and their wives. All reclined on richly decorated mats and cushions.

Attendants dragged around heavy leather trays heaped with roasted horsemeat, boiled mutton, rice dishes, and fruit. The women of Timur's household, their faces painted stark white, appeared wearing huge, heavy, plumed and embroidered headdresses set with pearls, rubies, and turquoise. Great jugs of wine stood ready along the paved garden paths for it was customary to drink large quantities before eating and considered a sign of manliness to become drunk.

To create his grand city, Timur brought in the master builders and architects of Persia. From India he brought in stone masons and even elephants to haul the stone. He envisioned Samarkand as a center of trade and culture: therefore, the builders were joined by gem cutters, craftsmen who made glass, porcelain, silver; and painters, physicians and learned men from many lands. To modernize his army he imported gunsmiths and bow makers from Turkey, and the armorers who made the famous Damascene blades. Examples of some of the minor arts of Timur's Samarkand have survived, but there are no paintings which would provide us with a pictoral reference to his court life. Timur was illiterate and may not have encouraged the art of the manuscript.

Clavijo estimated the polyglot population of Samarkand at 150,000, and reported that it was swelling so rapidly that the city and nearby villages were unable to house the newcomers: "hence they were to be found quartered temporarily for lodgment even in the caves and in tents under the trees of the gardens, which was a matter very wonderful to see."[11]

With Timur's victories, new fame came to Samarkand. It was soon known as a city of gardens, though the custom of building gardens had long been well established there. Tenth-century Arab geographers found the gardens so dense that the city appeared to be a mass of trees when viewed from the fortress heights.

Over three hundred years after the Arabs' account, Clavijo recorded that the city had the same appearance: "... Round and about the great men of the government also here have their estates and country houses, each standing within its orchard; and so numerous are these gardens and vineyards surrounding Samarqand that a traveller who approaches the city sees only a great mountainous height of trees and the houses embowered among them remain invisible."[12]

Samarkand may well have been the first garden city. As such, it differed greatly from Isfahan, built almost 250 years later. There was a unity in Shah Abbas's design for Isfahan with an axial plan centered on the avenue: Chahar Bagh and

Samarkand. Courtyard garden of Madrassa.

the gardens were contiguous. No integrated design or overall scheme is apparent in medieval plans of Timur's Samarkand. Though the individual chaharbaghs were geometrically laid out in the Persian style, the relationship of the gardens to each other and to the city appears casual. It may be that Timur planned his gardens to take advantage of some unusual natural feature in the landscape, such as a spring or a hill. He may have built them on the sites of older gardens or merely chose the site of encampments. Water was generally available: several streams ran through the meadows south of the Zerafshan river and Timur repaired and greatly enlarged the network of canals which irrigated the cultivated land outside of Samarkand, so it is unlikely that water determined the location of his gardens. Today a modern city has risen on the meadows which ringed the old city; though some fine examples of Timurid architecture remain, none of the gardens has survived.

A remark attributed to Timur claims that he owned the largest of all gardens—the valley of Soghd, the fertile area watered by the Zerafshan river between Samarkand and Bukhara. This was mentioned by some authorities in the tenth century as one of the "four earthly paradises" of the Muslims: the others were

Samarkand. Gur Amir. Timur's tomb with bulbous, blue-tiled, ribbed dome.

the Ubullah Canal gardens near Basra in the Tigris-Euphrates delta, the garden lands of Damascus, and the vale of Bavvan in Fars.[13]

The glacial waters of the Zerafshan flow westward and gradually diminish until they disappear completely in the black sands of the Kara Kum desert beyond Bukhara. Until recent years, this ancient city was totally dependent upon canals from the river for its water supply. For centuries, Bukhara was a major caravan center on the silk route and prospered as a large trading center for slaves.

In 1221, Jenghiz Khan is said to have stood on the steps of the Great Mosque of Bukhara and ordered "his troops to find fodder for their horses, i.e., gave permission to loot; and for days they indulged in an orgy of rape, plunder and destruction."[14] Although this sacking left Bukhara a dusty, smoking ruin, it recovered. When Maffeo and Nicolo Polo, the father and uncle of Marco Polo, sought refuge here in 1262 they thought it a large and splendid city. They were forced to remain for three years during a struggle for succession between the descendants of Jenghiz. It was in Bukhara where the Venetian merchants met the envoy of Kublai, the Khan of Cathay, and joined his homeward caravan, thus becoming the first Europeans to travel to the East.

Timur rebuilt the canals of Bukhara, constructed wells and markets, and his grandson Ulugh Beg built beautiful mosques and madrassas. Bukhara regained its reputation as a cultural center.

Timur coveted the lands of the eastern Khans and in 1405, old and feeble, he set out to invade Cathay, only to die in the winter snows on the steppes. At his death, his rule extended from the borderlands of the Mongols to the Mediterranean, and he had conquered Georgia and India.

Timur had used fear to rule his empire; his strict code of law was quickly and violently enforced. The submission of cities and states throughout the realm was retained only by the force of his iron rule and disappeared with his death. Only one hundred years later, in 1507, his only ruling descendant was the twenty-two-year-old Babur in Kabul. As the sole Timurid occupying a throne, Babur adopted the title Padshah, meaning "protecting lord" or "supreme." With this gesture, the youthful king asserted his supremacy over the clans of the Chagatis and Timurids. Vainly disputed by some rebel Timurids, his superiority became undeniable with his conquest of Hindustan. From that time the title Padshah came to mean emperor and was used by the Mughals of India.

Detail from the *Babur-Nama*.
(British Museum)

SEVEN

Babur

In the century following Timur's death in 1405, his provinces in Central Asia split into dozens of petty states; even so, there were more Timurid princes competing to rule than there were thrones to occupy. Lacking an exclusive right to inheritance, the strongest sword in a family or a clan often won the crown. Zahir-ud din Muhammad Babur was only twelve years old when his father, the local ruler of the rich valley of Ferghana northeast of Samarkand, died in a fall from his pigeon tower. Already a warrior, Babur won the throne.

Descended from Jenghiz Khan through his mother and from Timur on his father's side, Babur was certain he was destined to rule. This certainty never dimmed though in the next nine years he lost Ferghana, won and lost Samarkand twice, and was forced to seek his fortune south of the Oxus. Throneless, homeless, and penniless, he made his way across the Pamir Range and down through the Hindu Kush, and in 1504 took Kabul with a small, ragged band of loyal followers. It became his favorite province and remained his capital until his death.

Though it was an age of brutality, Timurid princes were often cultivated and accomplished; among them were astronomers, poets, musicians, and painters. Babur was a celebrated poet and musician who wrote in two languages. His character and life are well known from contemporary histories and his extraordinary autobiography, the *Babur-Nama*, is a warm and candid memoir, written with detachment and self-awareness. Keenly sensitive to his natural environment, he had the instincts of a naturalist; among his creative gifts was a talent for design. Utilizing these resources, he built a number of innovative gardens.

He had been dazzled by Samarkand, and the vision of it was always in his mind as he beautified Kabul: "Few towns in the whole habitable world are so pleasant as Samarkand."[1] Though he praised many royal chaharbaghs and meadows, he admired one garden most for its beauty, air and view, "Moreover, it was arranged symmetrically, terrace above terrace and is planted with beautiful *narwan*[2] and cypresses and white poplars. A most agreeable sojourning place, its one defect is the want of a large stream."[3] Steep terracing became characteristic of his design, and he apparently never built a garden without water.

In 1506, Babur spent a few months in Herat visiting his elegant relatives where he admired their refined manners and clever conversations. At this time, Herat was far more culturally and architecturally impressive than Samarkand, and it also must have had great influence on Babur's future building.

How he loved Kabul! The Kabul valley is near the crest of the Hindu Kush where the main ridge rises to peaks of over 20,000 feet. Babur traveled over every mountain; he knew every narrow defile and high pass. He rafted on all the rivers, and tasted all the fruit. He found the best meadows for horses and wooded slopes for game; and he knew the tiresome roads, where to avoid swarms of mosquitoes, and the rivers' fording places in all seasons. He knew the camping spots of all the nomads who followed their irregularly drifting flocks of sheep. He knew the legends, fears, crops and quirks of all the tribespeople, and watched the caravans wend their way northward from Hindustan to the Oxus and beyond.

He took pleasure in everything about Kabul and most especially loved its fine climate: "If the world has another so pleasant, it is not known. Even in the heats, one cannot sleep at night without a fur coat. Although the snow in most places lies deep in winter, the cold is not excessive."[4]

He rode through every village, and he always halted in a garden; if none existed, he created one. Or he embellished one such as he found outside the village of Istalif:

> ... There is a pleasant halting place outside it, under great planes, green, shady and beautiful. A one-mill stream, having trees on both banks, flows constantly through the middle of the garden; formerly its course was zig-zag and irregular; I had it made straight and orderly; so the place became very beautiful. Between the village and the valley bottom, from four to six miles down the slope, is a spring, known as Khwaja Sih-yaran (Three Friends), round which three sorts of tree grow. A group of planes gives pleasant shade above it; holm-oak grows in masses on the slope at its sides,—these two oaklands excepted, no holm-oak grows in the mountains of western Kabul,—and the Judas-tree is much cultivated in front of it, that is towards the level ground,—cultivated there and nowhere else.... I ordered that the spring should be enclosed in mortared stone-work 10 by 10, and that a symmetrical, right angled platform should be built on each of its sides, so as to overlook the whole field of Judas-trees. If, the world over, there is a place to match this when the arghwans are in full bloom, I do not know it.
>
> In order to bring water to a large round seat which I had built on the hillside and planted round with willows, I had a channel dug across the slope from a half-mill stream, constantly flowing in a valley to the south-west of Sih-yaran. It became a very good halting place. I had a vineyard planted on the hill above the seat...[5]

The site at Istalif is breathtaking. Two spurs jut from the mountain; the road curves up the steep grade, cuts through the garden on the first spur and winds its way to the village on the next. Raisins are the important crop of the area, and the valley between the spurs and the slopes below the village are thick with vineyards. Irrigation ditches snake along the base of the poplar trees planted between the rows of vines.

Babur directing the building of the watercourse at Shi-Yaran. From the *Babur-Nama*. (British Museum)

At the point where the road cuts across the first spur, a terrace stretches out onto a promontory which has a wonderful view of the broad valley and the mountains enclosing it. Just beyond the road, Babur's old watercourse still runs straight down the center of the terrace. Magnificent old chenars, at least twenty feet around, edge the terrace. At their base, about eighteen inches above the level of the terrace, are grass platforms—an old Timurid practice—hard with the gnarled roots of the aged trees.

Unobserved and unsuspected from the road, the garden rises up to the top of the mountain, "terrace above terrace" symmetrically, steeply rising—just as Babur preferred. The depression of the watercourse is still there. There are a few square pools on the narrow upper terraces, and some bits of cut stone, but little of the dressed stone facing remains. However, the absence of the facing reveals the construction of the terraces; heavy stones—blocks almost—were piled up,

81

followed by a layer of smaller, rougher stones placed more loosely with earth packed between and on top of them.

The highest terrace is the summit of the mountain. The level area ringed by trees has a panoramic view, which after the steep climb is exhilarating.

There are some graves in this Istalif garden. One is marked by a particularly handsome, small marble stone. Is it possible that Babur buried his mother here? She loved her warm-hearted, adventurous son and chose to share the privations of his rootless years. Sadly, she lived less than a year after reaching the security of Kabul. He wrote that he buried her in the New Year's garden built by Aulugh Beg Mirza; and he had bought the Istalif garden from the Mirza's descendants.[6]

Not too far away in a gully by the road, a huge old tree shades a torrent rushing down the hillside to the valley floor. There is a strange stone construction at the spot, obviously rebuilt, its original purpose now obscure. The hillsides are ridged by vineyards. The halting place Sih-yaran, perhaps?

There is much research to be done before positive identification can be made of many old garden sites. Place names have changed, spelling is unreliable, the landscape has been altered drastically by deforestation, and even rivers have changed their course. The very name "Kabul" has new meaning; now limited to the city, in Babur's time, it referred to a large province.[7]

Of all the gardens that Babur built, the best known today is the Bagh-i Wafa. His description of it states: "I laid out the Four-gardens, known as the Bagh-i-

Istalif. Huge old chenars with thick grass mounds at base.

82

Wafa (Garden of Fidelity), on a rising ground, facing south and having the Surkh-rud between it and Fort Adinapur. There oranges, citrons and pomegranates grow in abundance . . . . I had plantains brought and planted there; they did very well. The year before I had had sugar cane planted there; it also did well . . . . The garden lies high, has running-water close at hand, and a mild winter climate. In the middle of it, a one-mill stream flows constantly past the little hill on which are the four garden plots. In the south-west part of it there is a reservoir, 10 by 10, round which are orange-trees and a few pomegranates, the whole encircled by a trefoil-meadow. This is the best part of the garden, a most beautiful sight when the oranges take colour. Truly that garden is admirably situated!"[8]

This was written within the first year of his taking Kabul, and the garden became a regular halting place for him. Fifteen years later, he camped in the Garden of Fidelity for three or four days to enjoy the autumn ripening of the pomegranates: "Those were the days of the garden's beauty; its lawns were one sheet of trefoil; its pomegranate-trees yellowed to autumn splendour, their fruit full red; fruit on the orange trees green and glad, countless oranges had not yet as yellow as our hearts desired!"[9]

The Adinapur mentioned by Babur, in the passage about the Bagh-i Wafa, was located near the old city of Jalalabad. The city lies in a fertile valley 4,000 feet below Kabul, north of the Khyber Pass which leads down to the Indus Valley. The entire city is like a large, fragrant orange grove and the sugar cane introduced by Babur still thrives in large gardens on the edge of the city. One of these is believed to be the Bagh-i Wafa. It is as lovely a site as he described and might well be Babur's garden, but because of rebuilding through the years it defies positive identification without structural examination.

Jalalabad is an historic halting place on the route of invasion between the north and India. It has been identified with the city of Nysa visited by Alexander in 329 B.C. Then the citizens claimed it had been founded by Dionysus the Theban and took Alexander to "behold the mountain full of ivy and laurel, with all sorts of groves . . . . The Macedonians were delighted to see the ivy, since they had seen none for a long time; for there is no ivy in the Indians' country, not even where they have vines."[10]

Babur's route north to Kabul, which came to be known as the Mughal route when followed by his descendants, took him through the Jugdulluk Pass west of Jalalabad, rather than the modern route directly north through the Kabul Gorge. The old Mughal route is barely discernible today as it crosses an absolutely treeless desert; the land is not sand or soil but large stones. Twenty-five miles from Jalalabad, suddenly dense green cypress spires tower above the tall mud walls of a garden. It is the old Mughal garden of Nimla. At the sight of the trees, with the promise of flowing water and a green and fragrant world within, travelers automatically hasten, spurred on to the Paradise of the garden.

Some accounts say Babur built Nimla after he took Kabul in 1504; others say it was laid out by his great grandson, the emperor, Jahangir in 1610. In his *Memoirs*, Jahangir mentions a hunt arranged for him near Nimla while he camped in the Bagh-i Wafa in 1607.[11]

Nimla is unique among surviving Mughal gardens; it is the only garden where the planting is still Mughal. As we shall see in a later section, architectural features in the other surviving gardens often remain unchanged, but all the

Babur directing the building of the Bagh-i Wafa. Note engineer holding plan of garden, and workmen measuring plot. (Victoria and Albert Museum)

plantings have been greatly altered. In Nimla the architectural elements—stone watercourses, fountains, pavilions—are gone, but the planting is as it was originally. Here the bed of the watercourse is bordered by rows of chenars and cypresses, and there are plantations of orange trees in the plots. The ground beneath them is still carpeted with narcissus; the scent is dizzying.

The beauty of the glossy foliage and blossoms of the narcissus softens the rigid geometric layout of the plots which are bordered by enormous cypress trees, dense as a wall, and by chenars. The great old trees crowd and muscle each other for room. Some chenars are totally hollow, and the huge shells are deteriorating, though they still bear leaves. These trees do not seem to wither, die, and fall as others do—they literally disappear. Perhaps that is why they were thought to have magic properties, for it is a wonder that such hollow shells produce large colorful leaves.

It was an age of uncertainty and Babur did not have much leisure time to enjoy his gardens; he was confronted with the growing power of the Uzbeks in Central Asia. Kabul became crowded with Timurid refugees, their relatives and retainers; Babur's mountainous domains could not support his increasing number of dependents. Walled in by the Himalayas to the east, the powerful Uzbeks to the north and the Persian Shah to the west, he turned south for land to conquer. On his fifth and most daring attempt, he won the decisive battle for Hindustan.

While absent in India, Babur maintained Kabul as a crown domain, sending instructions to his governor in Kabul regarding his gardens: "...the avenue garden in which water is short and for which a one-mill stream must be diverted." Of one garden he had laid out but left unfinished, "the best of young trees must be planted there, lawns arranged, and borders set with sweet-herbs and with flowers of beautiful colour and scent." [12]

Babur died in India in 1530; his body was temporarily buried in his garden at Agra and was later brought to Kabul. As he wished, Babur has no great tomb but a simple grave marked by a marble stone erected by Jahangir. [13] The last phrase of the inscription reads: "Paradise is forever Babur Padshah's abode."

It is not certain what name Babur gave the garden which is now his grave site; Kabulis simply refer to it as "Babur's gardens." In the *Padshah-nama*, the history of the first ten years of Shah Jahan's reign, the garden is described as having fifteen terraces totaling 500 yards in length. The grave was on the fourteenth terrace, and a watercourse cascaded from the twelfth down through the remaining terraces. It was in a state of great disrepair, and Shah Jahan ordered the waterchannels rebuilt and edged with Kabul marble along with the construction of three large pools. In 1638, on the terrace below the grave, he erected a small, simple but elegant marble mosque.

Nimla. Railings are modern additions, but huge old cypress trees and broad walks flanking the watercourse are the original.

85

Today the sweeping central view down the terraces reveals little of the old Mughal character. European influence now dominates in the open space, hedges and reconstructed pools. The borders of cypress trees are gone, though plantations of trees in symmetrical rows still fill some plots of the broad terraces. Near Babur's grave there are some old chenars, one of which is quite extraordinary—more than forty-five feet in circumference. Kabulis believe it was planted by Babur, which would make it over 450 years old!

Having settled in Agra after winning the battle for Hindustan, Babur longed for Kabul; however, when some of his *Begs*, or chieftains, proposed returning, he responded passionately in words which not only reveal his character, but graphically describe his career: "There is no supremacy and grip on the world without means and resources; without lands and retainers, sovereignty and command are impossible. By the labours of several years, by encountering hardship, by long travel, by flinging myself and the army into battle, and by deadly slaughter, we, through God's grace, beat these masses of enemies in order that we might take their broad lands. And now what force compels us, what necessity has arisen that we should, without cause, abandon countries taken at such risk of life? Was it for us to remain in Kabul, the sport of harsh poverty? Henceforth, let no well-wisher of mine speak of such things!" [14]

There is no record of a European having met Babur; neither traveling merchant from Venice nor British adventurers made their way to Kabul or Agra during his reign. In Europe at this time, Henry VIII was watching Francis I and Charles V in preparation for choosing sides. It is not likely that any of these monarchs knew of Babur, though their descendants came to envy the great Mughals of India.

Kabul. View from the third terrace down central axis of garden.

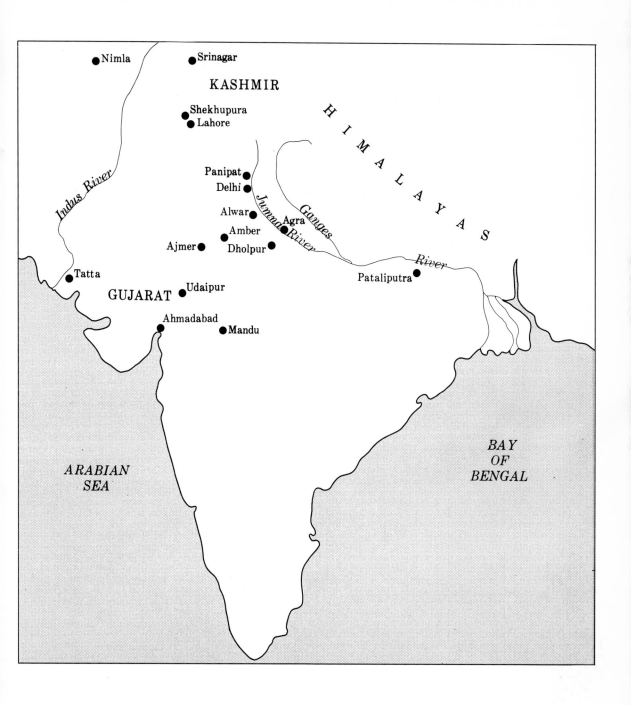

INDIA

EIGHT

The Indian Background

The great Indus River is generally identified with the Phison, one of the four biblical rivers of Paradise. From its source in the glaciers on the northern slopes of the central Himalayas, the Indus winds south and west almost 2,000 miles to the Arabian Sea. The most holy river of India, the Ganges, is formed of several Himalayan streams and flows south and east to the Bay of Bengal. In the foothills of the 1,500-mile double wall of the lofty Himalayas, the two great river systems and the wide Indo-Gangetic Plain form what was known in medieval times as Hindustan and what later became the Mughal Empire. Below the vast alluvial Plain, the high triangular tableland of the peninsular juts south into the Indian Ocean. Formed of many irregular ranges, it is bordered by crags and edged with two ribbons of sand—one of white, the other coral—which meet at Cape Comorin.

The Indus remains wide and deep throughout the year, but many rivers of northern India drop sharply or disappear altogether in the searing heat of summer. They are replenished by the summer monsoon which accounts for 70 percent of the country's rainfall. Before the canals and mechanized wells, when crops were totally dependent on the southwest monsoon, its failure meant a prolonged cycle of drought, famine, and pestilence.

About the middle of the second millennium B.C., the Aryans came from the northwest and overran the cities of the Indus valley. Since that time, the protective wall of the Himalayas has been penetrated repeatedly by invaders threading through the western passes. The Indus formed a second and often more effective barrier. Though the river was successfully crossed by Alexander and in spite of victories in the Punjab, the land of the five rivers, the discovery of the endless plain stretching before them so discouraged his troops they forced him to turn back. Thus the Macedonian conqueror abandoned his goal of reaching an eastern ocean. It was not until the medieval Muslim invasions that the Indus was again crossed by a foreign army.

Unlike the high, dry Persian plateau, the hills of ancient India were covered with lush vegetation, and the fertile Indo-Gangetic plain produced a rich agriculture. Attitudes toward nature and enclosures differed, and though—as we have seen—there was much cultural borrowing between the Indus Valley and Persia, the custom of Persian gardens had not been adopted in India. The building of such geometrically-planned, water-oriented Paradise gardens by the Mughals was an achievement, as the land, the climate and the culture of Hindustan were incompatible with such a garden tradition.

Historically, the Indians lived in communion with nature, but did not impose a symmetry upon it. A love of flowers and a reverence for trees and water were universal in India as in Persia and Central Asia. However, because of the different climatic conditions, cultural backgrounds and the absence of a custom of artificial waterways for irrigation, enclosed gardens marked by strong axial plans did not exist.

Climate and the land so govern human existence in India that they have been elemental forces in the development of the culture and even in shaping the character of the people. Indeed, the subcontinent is rich with a "full sacred geography. The living landscape is dense with significance." Professor Diana Eck observes that sacred literature frequently mentions holy places, "the Naimisa forest, the Ganga, Yamuna and Godavari rivers, the Himalaya and Vindhya mountains. Such places have been affirmed to have particularly strong strands of connection to the macrocosm. They are called *tirthas*, a word which originally meant 'ford' or 'crossing place' and has come to mean a 'spiritual ford, a place of pilgrimage.' "[1]

A network of thousands of tirthas unites diverse India as a cultural unit, Professor Eck continues: "Its unity as a nation ... has been firmly constituted by the sacred geography it has held in common and revered; its mountains, forests, rivers, hilltop shrines, and sacred cities."

Water is significant in Hindu mythic tradition and essential in the performance of religious ritual. The sacred river Ganga (Ganges), which has such immense cultural and religious significance to Hindus, had its mythic origins in the Vedas as a celestial stream flowing upon Earth.[2]

Various methods of collecting, storing, and conserving water have been used in India since Antiquity. Ancient storage tanks and wells are found everywhere. Water mills were apparently introduced in the eleventh century by a Persian who went to live an ascetic life among Brahman priests.

From ancient times, priests in India have maintained groves of flowering trees at temple sites; the blossoms are used in religious ritual. Certain trees and flowers were thought to symbolize the deities or to possess qualities which could enhance man's spiritual life. Planting a tree was an act of piety.

Such was the sacred Bo-tree under which Gautama, the Buddha, attained perfect knowledge. There is a legend that in the third century B.C., before his conversion to Buddhism, the great Asoka burned this sacred wild fig tree, and it was miraculously reborn from its own ashes. In the seventh century A.D., a cutting from this tree was the greatest gift the Indian king could send to the emperor of China. Another mighty Indian fig, the Banyan tree, which marvelously creates the effect of an arbor by sending many shoots down from its lower branches, is a

Detail from the Bharhut stupa, second
century B.C, showing Buddhist enclosure
with sacred tree being venerated.
(Indian Museum, Calcutta)

Ganga personified as a goddess.
Fifth-century terra cotta. Note symbolic
water pot.   (National Museum of India,
New Delhi)

holy tree to the Hindus. Tulsi was the holy basil of the Hindus, planted in memory
of deceased relatives.

An archaic religious symbol, the lotus was adopted by the invading Aryans.
Identified with Lakshmi, the lotus is also the cushion, pedestal or throne of Shiva;
and Brahma, the God-creator, is shown on a thousand-leaved lotus. The lotus
became closely identified with the Buddha, usually seated on the blossom, and
a goddess with a lotus and a water jug is seen at the Buddhist shrine of Sanchi.[3]

Hindu myths abound in floral imagery: seed of woe, fruit of wisdom, and a
charming myth about the mango tree as the daughter of the Sun God. There is
infrequent reference to secular gardens in Indian literature, although the *Kama-
sutra*, which records life 2,000 years ago, describes four gardens.

One garden was reserved for kings and queens, according to Professor M. S.
Randhawa, who writes that in the second garden the king played games such as
chess and was entertained by jesters. The third garden was where ministers and

Pataliputra, third century B.C. Colossal capital recovered from excavations that revealed the existence of pillared halls which rivaled "the splendor of Susa," to quote Megasthenes.

courtiers made merry with courtesans, and the fourth was dedicated to Lord Indra. In addition to geese, ducks, and swans splashing on the ponds, peacocks strutted under the trees which held gilded cages with colorful birds. No garden was complete without a swing.[4]

The oldest Western description of an Indian garden is found in the fragments of Megasthenes' record of his embassy to the Mauryan court about 300 B.C. The founder of the Mauryan Dynasty, Chandragupta, was the fist native Indian leader to gain control of all Hindustan when he forced Alexander's successor, Seleucus, to withdraw beyond the Indus. Seleucus sent his friend, Megasthenes, to Pataliputra (modern Patna), Palimbotra to the Greeks, the splendid, fortified Mauryan capital. Megasthenes described the richly painted, columned palace and royal garden:

> In the parks tame peacocks are kept, and pheasants which have been domesticated; and among cultivated plants there are some to which the king's servants attend with special care, for there are shady groves and pasture-grounds planted with trees, and branches of trees which the art of the woodsman has deftly interwoven. And these very trees, from the unusual benignity of the climate, are ever in bloom, and, untouched by age, never shed their leaves; and while some are native to the soil, others are with circumspect care brought from other parts, and with their beauty enhance the charms of the landscape. The olive is not of the number, this being a tree which is neither indigenous to India, nor thrives when transported thither . . . . Within the palace grounds there are also artificial ponds of great beauty in which they keep fish of enormous size but quite tame. No one has permission to fish for these except the king's sons while yet in their boyhood. These youngsters amuse themselves without the least risk of being drowned while fishing in the unruffled sheet of water and learning how to sail their boats.[5]

This scene could be a description of an Achaemenid pairidaeza. Indeed, the western provinces of the Indus valley had been annexed to his empire by Darius I. It was the marvelous accounts of this twentieth satrapy which fired Alexander's imagination and led to his invasion of India.[6] In his chronicle on Alexander's Eastern campaign, Pliny wrote that the young Macedonian leader greatly admired the trees of India, particularly the magnificent peepul tree. Pliny,

91

Sanchi, *ca.* second to first
century B.C. Yakshi on east gate.

however, was puzzled by the already profitable Indian commerce in pepper "which grew wild everywhere," and which he felt had "nothing to recommend it either for fruit or berry, its pungency being the only quality for which it is esteemed."[7] Strabo found the Indian trees remarkable, "among others one having branches which bend downwards, and leaves which are not less in size than a shield."

Little is known of other ancient Indian gardens after Megasthenes' description of Pataliputra. Centuries later, Arab writers describe the western port of Cambay as having lovely gardens and being "the first city of Hind." But Cambay's harbor silted up, commerce failed, and its great gardens, if they existed, are buried in the sand which covers the ancient city.

Arab traders had visited the coastal cities of India for centuries before the eleventh century when Muslim armies from the north invaded India. The rich Indian culture was singularly and pervasively religious. With their prohibition against representational art, the Muslims regarded the Hindu and Jain symbols of gods as idols and their religion as pagan. For the Indians, the temple was the historic center of life and the purpose of art was religious—to give physical characteristics to abstract spiritual concepts and to help man attain unity with the divine. The human forms used as symbols of the deities were intended not to imitate the forms of nature, but to represent its spirit. The free expression of this intense naturalism in Indian art resulted in an inevitable and fundamental conflict with the iconoclastic, monotheistic Muslim invaders.

Arab spice traders had visited the port cities for centuries, and some Muslim merchants had settled in the major cities, but the first successful Muslim invaders came by land from the north and west, plundering in the name of their religion and making frequent destructive raids on temples. In the twelfth century, the northerners stayed and established rule in the provinces skirting the mountains. The first buildings these invaders erected were mosques, usually of material from destroyed temples; as they became more secure in their rule, they built other structures of new material and developed an identifiable architectural style.

As we have seen, Islamic architecture was essentially Persian—brick and rubble construction with tile decoration. The structural principle was one of arcuation; it employed arches of dressed stone set in lime mortar to span spaces.

Since the time of Ashoka in the mid-third century B.C., the building material in pre-Muslim Indian architecture was stone, and the structural principle was simple gravity: the thrust of weight was vertically downward, and mass was required to support weight. In application, this principle was based on trabeation: spaces were bridged by horizontal beams, or post and lintel construction in imitation of forms established earlier in wood. Arrian, quoting Megasthenes, confirms that before Ashoka the Indians built their cities of wood "for if they were built of brick, they could not last long because of the rain," and that only "such cities as are built on high and lofty places, they make of brick and clay."[8]

The arch was well known to these early mathematicians; in fact, crude stepped or corbelled arches were used in the brick buildings of the Indus valley civilization.[9] Low domes appeared frequently. Most buildings were constructed for religious purposes and were meant to last indefinitely; therefore trabeation was preferred because it provided greater strength. Massive stone courses were cut and fit, and small amounts of mortar were used—for a more perfect fit rather than as a bonding material.[10] The Indians had a genius for the sculptural treatment of a building surface and created color effects by carving.

The structural principles of the Muslims, when executed in stone by native Indian craftsmen, produced the distinctive Indo-Islamic style of architecture. This style was quite mature by the sixteenth century when Babur invaded Hindustan, but it reached its perfection in the Mughal designs.

Architecture in India was customarily treated as one of the building crafts; a building was always the collective effort of several guilds, and few master builders have been identified. Guilds were established as early as the second century B.C. Men worked from intricate, ancient rules, memorized and passed from one generation to the next as membership became hereditary. Few written plans existed. The traditional methods were conservative, the tools very limited. Stonemasons had no drills, but used wooden wedges, hammers, and various sized iron chisels. Within the guilds, workers were ranked by skill. "Tracers" worked on designs, "plain cutters" and laborers quarried. At that time, a sculptor was little more than a tracer, and they essentially did the same work.

The stones were cut to exact size, and often sculpted, in the quarry. The finished stones were brought to the temple site and assembled. There was also an ancient tradition of rock-cut temples. Excavated from the natural rock, these temples were more sculpture than architecture, and the stonemasons who carved them more artists than artisans. Monumental stone structures were almost always temples, since it was not customary in India to build monuments to the dead.

Of the provincial architectural styles which developed in the belt of Muslim states across pre-Mughal Hindustan, the highest and most influential was that of Gujarat, a style that reflected not so much the taste or interest of the powerful

Ahmadabad. Kankariya Lake, 1451. A polygon of 34 sides, each 190 feet long. In the center was an island garden and the 72-acre lake was surrounded by gardens. No traces of them remain.

Muslim ruler as the unsurpassed skill of the native craftsmen. These Gujarati workmen introduced a naturalistic element into the decoration of Muslim buildings throughout the north. Appealing to the strong feeling for naturalism in the Mughals, naturalistic form became a dominant aspect in Mughal design.

It has been suggested that in pre-Mughal Muslim India, the native Hindu workmen deliberately incorporated ancient Hindu motifs into the decoration of Muslim buildings, and that these went unrecognized by the foreign rulers. Water and serpents are linked frequently in Hindu mythology, for legendary serpents called *Nagas* are believed to be guardians of springs and holy tanks, and are thought to dwell in the waters beneath the roots of holy trees.[11]

In the uninhabited central Indian city of Mandu there is a striking example of an ancient Hindu motif incorporated into a Muslim palace. Strategically located on a narrow plateau which juts one thousand feet above the surrounding plain, Mandu had been fortified since Antiquity. It became the capital of the Muslim state of Malwa in the fifteenth century. The city covered the twenty-square-mile area of the summit within massive walls. Successive Muslim rulers built impressive mosques and tombs and gay palaces and pavilions. The surface of the plateau is irregular with rocky outcrops, dense trees, springs and lakes, streams and ravines, and today has the look of a wild garden, deserted and seemingly suspended above the level landscape of the plain.

Built between two lakes, the narrow Jahaz Mahal, or ship palace, has rooftop *chhatris*, small open-sided pavilions with a cupola, which suggest the fanciful superstructure of a fairy-tale ship. A roof garden with an elegantly designed pool has a series of intricate water devices of intertwining serpents. A few miles away, nestled in a treacherously steep ravine at the edge of the palisade, is a small Mughal building over a spring with a pool and a similar water device. It was built around 1577 by an Amir of the Emperor Akbar. With the decline of the Mughals, *Nilkanth*, as the spring is known, became a tirtha of the Hindus where pilgrims collected water and left votive offerings.

The northern Sultanates of Hindustan were plagued with border raids by Mongols from Central Asia. The horde of Jenghiz Khan swept down through the mountains in 1221, but stopped at the Indus River. When Timur crossed the Indus in 1398, he left a trail of carnage along the route of his brief and bloody raid which was unequaled in India's long history. Timur's sack of Delhi crippled the Sultanate, which had formerly been a union of major Muslim states. Several powerful states broke away leaving behind a coalition of minor states which were politically fragmented by the rivalry and the constant changes in leadership. Persistent political instability made it possible for the adventurous Babur to defeat the Sultan of Delhi and his weak confederates in 1526.

pre-Mughal.

Mughal era.

Mandu. Serpent water devices

NINE

Babur: Conquest

The march from Kabul south took Babur's army five months with frequent camps and foraging, skirmishes and negotiations. Babur obviously enjoyed himself and observed and recorded everything—animals, birds, plants—and was in high spirits when he reached the Siwalik hills. Here, in February 1526, some weeks before his decisive victory at Panipat, in a confident gesture he laid out his first charbagh* in India.[1]

The area was famous in history and legend. One of the earliest regions settled by the Aryans and mentioned in the epic, the *Mahabharata*, it was the site of the holy river Saraswati of Vedic times. The rivers of northern India frequently changed course and several, including the Saraswati, have been lost in the sands of the desert. Today the entire watershed has been changed by canalization and, though sections of a deserted artificial stone waterway have been found above the Ghaggar River, the site Babur described cannot be identified.

In an interesting coincidence, the last great Paradise Garden of the Mughal era was built not far above this first garden. At the end of the seventeenth century, the Emperor Aurangzeb's foster brother and engineer, Fadai Khan, built the garden of Pinjaur on an old garden site in the hills near the Hindu shrine at Panchpura. Steeply terraced and fed by over 300 springs on the mountainside, it is one of the most joyous water gardens of the Mughals. A favorite Indian anecdote is attached to this garden: the Rana who ruled locally tricked the Mughals into abandoning Pinjaur by sending only women afflicted with goiter to work in the *zenana*, or women's, quarters. When these women claimed the water was responsible for their deformity, the frightened Mughal harem demanded to leave and refused to return.[2]

Babur continued moving southeast; in April his 8,000 troops faced 100,000 men and 1,000 war elephants of the Sultan of Delhi on the plain at Panipat.

---

*In India the preferred term for a four-fold garden is charbagh, using the Hindi word char which means four. Chahar is a Persian word.—E.B.M.

Babur's small, new artillery force and experienced, flexible cavalry easily confused and routed the cumbersome force of the vain and inexperienced Sultan. Victory was won for Babur by the swift and slender Central Asian horses he prized. Even when mortally wounded, these horses had been known to carry their masters to safety before they fell. The slaughter was excessive and for centuries the battlefield was said to be haunted at dawn. Even British travelers in the nineteenth century claimed to hear sounds of wailing and terror and the desolating fury of a battle.

Babur pushed on to Agra, which the ancestors of the defeated Sultan had made their capital, but found it a ghost city; the people had fled in fear. It was the hottest season in a year of drought, and Babur's northern troops loathed the violent sandstorms and fell ill in the fierce May heat. Food was scarce, fodder almost nonexistent. The heat of the level plain of northern Hindustan was as deadly for their mounts as for Babur's mountain men. He had to inspire and persuade his followers to remain.

Babur's was a turbulent life, given the enormous physical demands of a warrior and the burdens of rule in unsettled times, and he was often ill. He took great pleasure in planning his gardens; before he could turn his energies to them, however, he had to subdue the Hindu chieftains who had united under Rana Sanga of Mewar. In the last major battle of his life, he defeated the great Rajput warrior in March 1527.

Unlike his Central Asian ancestors, Babur was not a predatory raider, and he spent the remaining three years of his life in Hindustan trying to consolidate and unify the northern provinces. Propelled by his great natural curiosity, he learned all he could about his new domain. In his Memoirs, he wrote: "Hindustan is of the first climate, the second climate, and the third climate, of the fourth climate it has none. It is a wonderful country. Compared with our countries it is a different world; its land, its animals and plants, its peoples and their tongues, its rains and its winds, are all different.... Once the water of Sind (the Indus) is crossed, everything is in the Hindustan way land, water, tree, rock, people and horde, opinion and custom."[3]

Having lived through the cycle of the seasons in Hindustan, Babur felt "its air in the Rains is very fine ... torrents pour down all at once and rivers flow where no water had been. While it rains and through the Rains, the air is remarkably fine, not to be surpassed for healthiness and charm."[4]

As in Kabul, Babur's gardens in Hindustan were terraced, and their strong axial symmetry was dominated by the watercourse. However, the climate in Hindustan made it possible for him to expand his use of the gardens and thus broaden their function. Babur's inherited nomadic tendency was reinforced by a lifetime spent as a soldier, and he preferred to live in his charbaghs as Timur had rather than in the confined space of a palace. In Kabul, he had been restricted to the palace in the severe winter months; with the coming of spring, in keeping with the old Central Asian practice, he had moved to great encampments in gardens and meadows without the city.

In Hindustan, the extensive walled and terraced charbaghs Babur built were delightful open air palaces. Each terrace had a specific use which corresponded to certain rooms within a palace and included baths and a mosque. In his gardens, Babur planned military campaigns, held public audiences, wrote his memoirs, composed poetry and music, entertained, and reveled with his friends.

Persian wheel. "In Lahor, . . . and in those parts people water by means of a wheel. They make two circles of ropes long enough to suit the depth of the well, fix strips of wood between them, and on these fasten pitchers. The ropes with the wood and attached pitchers are put over the well wheel. At one end of the wheel axle a second wheel is fixed, and close to it another on an upright axle. This last wheel the bullock turns; its teeth catch in the teeth of the second, and, thus, the wheel with the pitchers is turned. A trough is set where the water empties from the pitchers, and from this the water is conveyed everywhere." Annette Susannah Beveridge, The *Babur-Nama* (London: 1969), p. 486.

The life of the ruler within the confines of the palaces was thus transposed to the gardens.

Babur's choice of sites and dramatic terracing testifies to his genius as a garden designer; he possessed the flair and spatial sense inherent in all Mughals. His basic design and use of his Paradise Gardens were merely modified by his successors. The introduction of marble as a building material in gardens built by Jahangir, and its wider use by Shah Jahan, changed the appearance of the garden, but not its basic design; its function remained essentially the same.

The Central Asian Mughals were the world's most elegant nomads; it is precisely this nomadic characteristic which explains the importance that their gardens held for them. The Mughals used their charbaghs as no other great dynasty has used gardens. Neither decorative adjuncts to a palace nor intended simply for visual enjoyment, gardens were used in place of buildings.

The most creative period in Mughal history were the years between 1526 and 1657, and includes the reigns of the first five emperors: Babur, Humayun, Akbar, Jahangir, and Shah Jahan. Of these, Babur and his great-grandson Jahangir were the most ardent nature lovers and the most prolific garden builders. Enamored of gardens, Babur's son, Humayan, often languished in them during his exile, but there are no detailed descriptions of any he built.

Akbar's genius was administrative: he consolidated the empire, established the Mughal government, and as a tireless builder, erected many great forts in northern Hindustan. Though gardens were included in the planning of these massive forts, they were not of special interest to Akbar. Jahangir, a born naturalist, was a passionate sportsman. He built the greatest number of Paradise Gardens, many of which were on his route of travel in search of game or pleasure. The last of this group of rulers, Shah Jahan, had enormous talent as an architect; though his first love was designing buildings, he built many gardens. Most surviving Mughal gardens are remnants of Shah Jahan's or were built by his nobles.

But for a few brilliant exceptions which took advantage of a natural feature in the landscape—such as the spring of Vernag in Kashmir—the Mughals built three types of gardens: those within palace courts, surrounding tombs, and large charbaghs or Paradise Gardens. They occasionally also built a few remote gardens such as Jahangir's hunting lodge at Sheikhupura, in what is now Pakistan; these were similar to the Pairidaeza of the Sassanian kings of Persia.

Sheikhupura. West of Lahore. Known as Jahangirabad when it was the hunting lodge of Jahangir.

Some Mughal Paradise Gardens, such as the Lotus Garden at Dholpur, thirty-five miles south of Agra, were within a day's trip of the capital or fort, and were enjoyed in much the same manner as Western rulers enjoyed their country houses or retreats. That any of these secular Paradise Gardens have survived the vicissitudes of time is due in good part to the excellence of their planning and construction. The preservation and restoration of the gardens, begun under Lord Curzon at the turn of the century, is supervised by the Archaeological Survey of India, and has been very carefully and well executed.[5] Today, with their pools empty and waterchannels dry, however, the spaces of the palace courts within the formidable walls of the fortress cities are forlorn and echoing.

The walled charbaghs surrounding the Imperial tombs have survived in the best condition. The use of large charbaghs on a single level as the setting for monumental tombs was the most important innovation in garden architecture by the Mughals who followed Babur.

These tomb gardens recalled an earlier Persian garden design where there were no terraces and only a slight slope and shallow changes in level for the gravity-fed water system. The overall scheme of the tomb gardens was square with a multiple division of plots in the four quarters. The usual plan of the Paradise Gardens was a parallelogram with four-square gardens on each terrace.

Water dominated Babur's gardens and those of all the later Mughals. The heart of their charbaghs was the central watercourse; the flowing water gave life to the garden. The early gardens were dependent upon wells; later, construction of canals drawn from major rivers provided a more dependable water supply. Then, watercourses became wider and were studded with fountains. These beguiling water gardens in a waterless landscape provided the viewer with a scene, at once sensuous and poetic.

The Mughals loved symbolism, and it was an important consideration in their garden design. Like the Muslim gardens of Persia and Central Asia, the terraces in the Mughal garden often represented those of the Koranic Garden of Paradise. Superstitious, as well as religious, some of the emperors sought guidance from the stars and occasionally built their charbaghs to conform to the number of planets, or signs of the Zodiac. As Timur had before them, these Timurids thought the number nine was auspicious for them.[6]

Eight was another number with special meaning for the Mughals, and the octagon was a favorite design in their early gardens for pools and platforms and even pavilions, although Shah Jahan usually used the square. The octagon as the circle squared—the circle symbolizing eternal perfection, the square symbolizing earthly order—represented man's wish for order.

We know from remaining sites, ruins, and contemporary descriptions that Babur's early gardens in Hindustan reflected his love of nature and were, like him, exuberant. These early Mughal gardens had more vitality and a stronger character than the later, more voluptuous gardens. After Akbar achieved political stability, power and riches accrued to the emperor. The ease resulting from such security and wealth was reflected in Mughal building. In later gardens, the structures became palatial; light silken awnings above platforms gave way to marble pavilions, as building materials became increasingly extravagant. The luxurious palaces in the forts were simultaneously influenced by garden design. This mutual influence of garden and palace culminated in Shah Jahan's palace in the Red Fort of Shahjahanabad at Delhi, which was not a palace at all but a terrace of luminous marble pavilions linked by gardens and watercourses.

As with the Persians, flowering fruit trees represented renewal. The cypress represented eternity to the Mughals and bordered the walks and waterchannels of their gardens. Orange and citron were also favored for these borders; pomegranates, almonds, and date palms were grouped in the plots. The fruits were not mixed, for different species required varying amounts of water and care. Beneath the groves of trees, masses of spring-flowering plants—iris, daffodils and narcissus—were preferred. In some later gardens, flower beds were occasionally planted with a single variety massed in a pattern that created a mosaic-like effect. Many hybridized roses were cultivated, and jasmine was a great favorite, especially in the strongly scented moonlight gardens.

The emperors all had a great fondness for fruit—for some it was practically an obsession—and they spared no effort to ensure that fresh fruit was brought to them from all parts of their empire. They introduced many new varieties to India; fruit trees from northern valleys—even those beyond Kabul—were transplanted to the parched plains.

It was customary for the emperors to assign an engineer from their personal staff to direct a building project. In some cases, these engineers designed the gardens as well. Babur, however, created his own garden designs, and Jahangir improved the ideas of his engineers. Both were gifted natural botanists with a special interest in plants and their placement within the gardens. Their fondness for flowers was shared by the other emperors, but flowers were not essential to the charbaghs they built; water was.

An imaginative use of water much admired by Babur was the Indian *baoli* or step well. Evolving from Hindu tradition, the baoli appears, at ground level, to be

Ahmadabad. Baoli, or step well, of Dada Hari, 1435. Three levels below ground with finely carved galleries above an octagonal well. (Archaeological Survey of India)

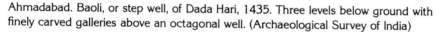

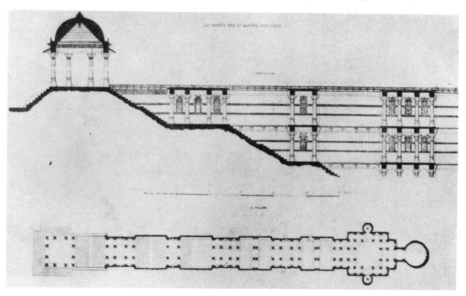

a garden pavilion. A flight of steps in the center, however, descends several stories to the underground water level. Each story consists of a gallery with rooms surrounding the central steps. These underground chambers remain cool and dark in the hot months before the monsoon. Babur constructed a "three storey" baoli within the old Lodi fort in Agra.[7] His example was followed by the later emperors who built baolis within their forts and many gardens in the hot plains.

The Lodi fort and the city of Agra, both taken by Babur in 1526, were built along the west bank of the Jumna River; the eastern bank was unsuitable because it was irregular, flat, and occasionally swampy. After searching for a suitable site for a great charbagh, however, Babur settled on the eastern bank. First, the land had to be reshaped: a massive, strongly reinforced masonry wall was constructed along the edge of the river, and heavy stones and earth were moved to the site for the foundations of the high riverfront terrace and elevated walkways.

"The beginning was made with the large well from which water comes for the Hot Bath, and also with the piece of ground where the tamarind-trees and the octagonal tank now are. After that came the large tank with its enclosure; after that the private-house with its garden and various dwellings";[8] Babur admired the tamarind's "finely cut leaves," and thought it "a very good-looking tree, giving dense shade. It grows wild in masses too."[9]

Persian wheels, known as *rehants* in India, were built into the corner towers of the supporting riverfront wall, with supplemental wells on a lower terrace. These fed the watercourses and pools, and their overflow irrigated the plots. The planting beds on the highest terrace were several feet below the elevated pathways. These plots held fruit trees, and strollers probably had the pleasing sensation of walking in the treetops.

Babur had "in every border rose and narcissus in perfect arrangement."[10] From the histories and journals of the time we learn that Babur loved the garden at Agra and lived in it. According to Jahangir, Babur "gave it the name of Gul Afshan (Gold Scattering) and erected in it a small building of cut red stone, and having completed a mosque on one side of it he intended to make a lofty building, but time failed him and his design was never carried into execution."[11]

When Babur's sons visited Agra after his death, they often lived in silken tents in his garden. Babur's grandson, Akbar, held public audience here in the early years of his reign. Almost ninety years after Babur's death, Jahangir inspected the garden regularly, and was once so pleased with its appearance that he generously rewarded the officer in charge.[12] Jahangir turned the Gul Afshan over to his adored queen, Nur Jahan, a lady of ambition, taste and talent, but not humility; she did not hesitate to change Babur's design.[13] Today it is generally believed that the garden called the Ram Bagh in Agra is the old Gul Afshan. The city has spread across the river, and dense traffic flows over what was once part of the garden; a commercial nursery flourishes on another section. A large portion of the riverfront terrace remains, but the buildings are those of Nur Jahan.

Babur's court had followed his example, and the banks of the holy Jumna flowered with luxuriant charbaghs. "The people of Hind," Babur wrote, "who had never seen grounds planned so symmetrically and thus laid out, called the side of the Jun where (our) residences were, Kabul."[14] Gardeners and men with special skills, such as in grafting trees, were brought from Persia and the north to tend these gardens and train local workers. In his Memoirs, Babur recalls his pleasure when a gardener from Balkh (now in Afghanistan) successfully raised melons in his Agra garden. Always experimenting with plants and introducing new cuttings, Babur had earlier planted vines there which he felt bore very good grapes.

Not just interested in the fruit, Babur also collected unusual flowers: "In these places the oleander-flower is peach, those of Gualiar are beautiful, deep red. I took some of them to Agra and had them planted in gardens there."[15]

Of the many buildings and gardens created by Babur near Kabul and in Hindustan, little remains. Of those that have survived, the Lotus Garden of Dholpur most clearly shows his design ideas. The walls are gone, the planting beds cannot be seen, but sections of the unique rock-cut complex—carved from a single outcropping of sandstone—survive, damaged but unaltered. Forgotten for almost four hundred years, the Lotus Garden was found and identified in March 1978 by the author.

Dholpur lies near the Chambal, a major river of Central India. Before being brought under control in the last century, the river's great flood tide dug a labyrinth of ravines, some 90 feet deep and extending four miles, into the alluvial soil which forms the exceptionally high banks—170 feet above the riverbed. Three miles south of the city is an ancient fording place below the hulking ruins of a fort said to be 3,000 years old. Because of its strategic location commanding the ford and the main route south, Babur made Dholpur a royal domain instead of assigning it to a local commander as was customary.

The plain west of Dholpur is broken by a dark red sandstone ridge which runs sixty miles to the northeast. The soil near the ridge is poor, an easily powdered friable alluvium mixed in places with stiff yellow clay. Because the land is

Agra. Ruined pavilions, remnants of Mughal gardens, along the Jumna River.

103

Square well of laid up stones, 10-by-10 gaz or roughly 23 feet square.

Aqueduct. Limestone waterway on dressed sandstone arches.

unproductive, it is sparsely settled, and the main route south still bypasses the Lotus Garden by several miles. This may explain why so much of the garden has survived, although much of the quarried stone used in some of the buildings has been carried away. A charming small village has been built on the level stone terraces, taking advantage of an elevated, solid base for the thatched-roof mud houses. The only tillable soil is that covering the former charbagh adjacent to the platform and the dry bed of the lake behind Sikandra Lodi's (1489–1517) ancient dam. It was at this dam, which crossed a small valley, that Babur stopped one August dawn in 1527. Seeing an unusually large outcropping of sandstone at the beginning of the ridge, he was sufficiently inspired to have a pavilion carved out of it—in one piece—and to design a garden around it.

During the next seventeen months, Babur visited Dholpur several times, personally supervising the construction of the Lotus Garden. Construction of the garden and Babur's involvement with the project and attention to detail are best learned from his own account:

September 1528: "That place is at the end of a beaked hill, its beak being of solid red building-stone. I had ordered the (beak of the) hill cut down to the ground-level and that if there remained a sufficient height, a house was to be cut out in it, if not, it was to be levelled and a tank cut out in its top. As it was not found high enough for a house, Ustad Shah Muhammad the stone-cutter was ordered to level it and cut out an octagonal, roofed tank. North of this tank the ground is thick with trees, mangoes, jaman, all sorts of trees; amongst them I had ordered a well made, 10-by-10;[16] it was almost ready; its water goes to the afore-named tank. To the north of this tank Sl. Sikander's dam is flung across (the valley); on it houses have been built, and above it the waters of the Rains gather into a great lake. On the east of this lake is a garden; I ordered a seat and four-pillared platform to be cut out in the solid rock on that same side, and a mosque built on the western one."[17]

October 4, 1528: "The face of the roofed-tank, ordered cut in the solid rock, was not being got up quite straight; more stone-cutters were sent for who were to make the tank-bottom level, pour in water, and, by help of the water, to get the

Hexagonal pool, 2 feet 5 inches in diameter, 6½ inches deep.

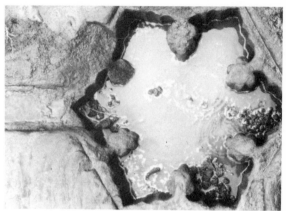

Hexagonal pool, 2 feet 6 inches in diameter, decorated with carved stone lotus buds.

sides to one height. They got the face up straight just before the Other Prayer, were then ordered to fill the tank with water, by help of the water made the sides match, then busied themselves to smooth them. I ordered a water-chamber made at a place where it would be cut in the solid rock; inside it was to be a small tank also cut in the solid rock." [18]

December 21, 1528: "On Thursday the 11th day of the month the stone-well, the twenty-six rock-spouts and rock-pillars and the water-courses cut on the solid slope were all ready. At the 3rd watch of this same day preparation for drawing water from the well was made. On account of a smell in the water, it was ordered, for prudence' sake, that they should turn the well-wheel without rest for 15 days-and-nights, and so draw off the water. Gifts were made to the stone-cutters, and labourers, and the whole body of workmen in the way customary for master-workmen and wage-earners of Agra." [19]

January 13, 1529: "On Thursday the 3rd of the first Jumada, a place was fixed in the s. e. of the garden for a Hot-bath; the ground was to be levelled; I ordered a plinth erected on the levelled ground, and a Bath to be arranged, in one room of which was to be a reservoir 10 × 10." [20]

In February, he made his last entry concerning the Lotus Garden, he gave leave to the master stone-cutter and to the "spadesman." [21]

The Lotus Garden has been declared a protected site by the Government of India and investigations are planned by the Archaeological Survey. At the time of this writing, however, the entire scheme of the garden is not clear. Footings for piers, some existing sections of dressed stone walls and other evidence suggest that a series of royal buildings stood on the main terrace overlooking the central pool. These included the emperor's small mosque; his rock-cut pavilion opposite it, and between the two at the back of the terrace, his private apartments. The mosque stood within a walled enclosure built of finely cut, fitted stone, with a building of the same construction beside it.

When the Lotus Garden was discovered, it was possible to trace the source and movement of water for only one of the three original waterchannels which fed into the large pool on the central terrace. [22] A round well, now shaded by a

105

Detail of foliated octagonal pool on main terrace, 29 feet in diameter. The watercourses cut in the terrace, 7 inches wide.

massive old tree, provided water for an aqueduct which carried it to a stone tank constructed at the edge of the platform. The tank fed two channels cut into the rock; one led to Babur's hot bath nearby, the other ran through the limestone paved mosque, spilled down a chaddar into a plain octagonal pool in the mosque forecourt, and overflowed into a channel which ran to a small, shallow octagonal pool at the edge of the platform. From this upper level, the water simply fell into a hexagonal pool on the central terrace; some flowed onto the large central pool, some ran off the platform most likely to water the planting beds below.

The Lotus Garden is the first example of the brilliant assimilation of Mughal design with Indian skill and creativity in garden architecture. Here in the barren desert, on a monolithic platform of living rock, is carved a series of pools depicting the ancient lotus symbol in various forms—bud, flower, and overripe blossom.

The small hexagonal pool below the mosque forecourt is decorated with tight foliation and lotus buds. The central octagonal pool represents an open lotus blossom, and the lower pool has lobed, widely separating lotus petals. In the lower pool, the lotus petal is carved in a positive-negative repeat; above the void of water, the substance of red stone must have given the effect of petals floating on the water.

The lotus pools on the central terrace are united by flowing water. A series of pools, developing a single theme, was a new concept. Although simple foliated pools were built by the Timurids at the end of the fourteenth century, such a sophisticated thematic plan is not known before this.

As we have seen, the adaptable form of the lotus had consistently recurred in the art and architecture of West Asia since ancient times. The lotus blossom symbolized the universe to the Hindus, and the wheel of law and the sun to the Buddhists, so its use as a basis for design in India is almost infinite.

The treatment of the lotus in the pools at Dholpur is distinctively Indian.

106

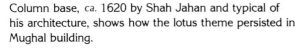
Each petal of lower lotus pool is 22 inches wide.

Column base, *ca.* 1620 by Shah Jahan and typical of his architecture, shows how the lotus theme persisted in Mughal building.

See back cover for waterchute.

Dholpur sandstone is finely grained, easily worked, and hardens by exposure to weather, but only master craftsmen skilled in the technique could carve the lotus designs in living rock. The dark, reddish-purple stone is effectively lightened by the flawless carving of the imaginative foliation.

Babur's hot bath still stands in almost perfect condition; it is used as a stable by a village family. Of Hindu slab construction, it is a plain, rectangular structure measuring slightly more than twelve- by twenty-two feet. Within the simple sandstone building is a deep, sunken bath of white stone. A narrow channel carried the overflow beneath the wall to an adjacent square tank of dressed stone.

As we have seen, Timurid garden pavilions in Persia and Central Asia were simple stone platforms which could accommodate decorative poles to support an elegant awning of rich, embroidered material. Larger structures were open, painted pavilions on raised platforms. We cannot be certain of the appearance of Babur's pavilions in Agra or in Dholpur. Illustrations in existing manuscripts of the *Babur-Nama* cannot be relied upon as guides as they were painted years after his death and the succeeding emperors never hesitated to rebuild existing gardens or palaces to their own design.

Given the Indian influence in the design of the pools and the Indian construction of the hot bath, it is possible that Babur's pavilions at Dholpur resembled chhatris. These are small open structures built of stone with bracketed pillars that support a roof—usually a cupola—with deep eaves. Later, they were frequently used by the Mughals to decorate rooftops, and they appear in some of their gardens.

Babur with attendants in a garden pavilion. Mughal, late sixteenth century. (Freer Gallery of Art)

Though it covers many acres, the exact size of the Lotus Garden is not known. The bleak desert to the west is dotted with abandoned Mughal wells, platforms, and at least one pavilion which is now a Hindu shrine. The surrounding area is rich in ruins from several earlier periods. Near the garden a large tank or catchment area is formed by three sets of stone steps each 100 feet long. The middle set of steps, with a large embankment built against them, forms a wall. On top of the embankment, stairs lead down to a bath house where flaking plaster on the walls reveals that the materials used in construction were taken from temples. This bath may pre-date the Mughals, for they did not use such materials.

A high, dark stone wall, possibly part of an old dam, runs several hundred yards along the southeast side of the garden. Collapsed upon it is a simple stone pavilion, its four columns and capitals unbroken but piled in a heap. Just beyond the end of this wall the skeletons of once grand buildings of pre-Mughal times are starkly silhouetted atop an old dam. Less than a mile away lies Mach Kund, a deep spring-fed lake surrrounded by over a hundred temples; the site of annual pilgrimages, it is deserted most of the year.

In her warm and lively Memoirs, Babur's daughter, Gul Badan, recalled that her father planned to fill the tank at Dholpur with wine when it was finished, but prior to its completion, he took an oath against wine, so he filled the tank with lemonade![23]

To those familiar with Mughal history in India today, Gul Badan's anecdote is well known and remembered with amusement, though the Lotus Garden itself was long-forgotten and was assumed to have disappeared. The villagers of Jhor had not heard of Gul Badan or her story, but in conversation after the discovery of the garden confirmed the connection. Though they were surprised to learn the site was Babur's garden, two old men gleefully related a village tale of his warriors filling the large pool with wine and getting drunk there.

Gul Badan tells a moving story of Babur's attempt to cheer his grieving wife on the death of their young son by taking the ladies of his family on an outing to the Lotus Garden. During this visit, he learned that another of his sons, Humayun, was ill and near death. Babur hastily returned to Agra where he soon fell ill and died. E. M. Forster, charmed by Babur's autobiography, wrote of his death: "Nothing in his life was Indian, except, possibly, the leaving of it. Then, indeed, at the supreme moment, a strange ghost visits him, a highly unexpected symptom occurs—renunciation.

"Humayun, his son, lay sick at Agra, and was not expected to recover. Babur, apprised that some sacrifice was necessary, decided (who told him?) that it must be self-sacrifice. He walked ceremonially three times round the bed, then cried, 'I have borne it away.' From that moment strength ebbed from him into his son, a mystic transfusion of the life-force was accomplished, and the five senses that had felt and discriminated so much blended together, diminished, ceased to exist, like the smoke from the burning ghats that disappears into the sky. Not thus had he faced death in the past. Read what he felt when he was nineteen, and his enemies closed round the upland garden in Ferghana. Then he was rebellious and afraid. But at fifty, by the banks of the sacred Jumna, he no longer desired to continue, discovering, perhaps, that the so-called Supreme Moment, is after all, not supreme, but an additional detail, like a cup that falls into the water, or a game of chess played with both hands, or the plumage of a bird, or the face of a friend."[24]

Babur's victory in Hindustan and his hold on the country were due directly to the strength of his personality, the force of his will and the affection and loyalty of his men. His life was a series of dramatic crises and spectacular achievements, and it was with some drama that he departed from it. Designer, builder, botanist and surely the greatest garden builder among kings, Babur's legacy is impressive: the tradition he established in Mughal India produced terraced water gardens which most resembled the ideal—the joyous, peaceful Garden of Paradise.

TEN

Humayun: Exile

The twenty-two-year-old Humayun (1530–1556), while not actively opposed as Babur's chosen successor, was resented by his younger more competent brothers and some strong followers of Babur. In spite of being brave and his training for leadership, Humayun was disturbingly indecisive, often idle, and self-indulgent. When opposed by Sher Shah, a descendant of Pathan rulers in India and a man of ability and energy, he could not muster the personal or military resources to defeat him. Barely escaping with his life, he spent several years in humiliating retreat—literally from garden to garden. On his flight to Persia in exhausted condition after a dreadful march across the desert of Sind through thick patches of thorn brake, Humayun reached the Paradise Gardens of the Arghuns above the Indus River. Among the earliest Timurid-style charbaghs on the subcontinent, they are mentioned frequently in history.

The Arghuns were among the many followers of Timur who competed for rule in small states. One, Maquim, had lost Kabul to the youthful Babur. Maquim's elder brother, Shah Beg Arghun, had pushed south and had established rule in the ancient city of Tatta which commanded much of the Indus delta.

To protect the Indus River approach to Tatta, the Arghuns strongly reinforced the unique island fort of Bakker, a six-day march to the north. They built a palace and laid out a royal garden on the mainland, opposite the fort. The entire area flowered into a shady, continuous charbagh when the nobles followed the princely example.

None of his brothers offered sanctuary to Humayun; they pursued him and drove him into exile in Persia where he sought help from Shah Tahmasp. The Shah provided the royal refugee with a splendid encampment in the Garden of Desire in Herat, and later welcomed him to his "paradise-like court" with flights of arrows and blaring trumpets, while surrounded by prostrate nobility.

The pious Tahmasp exacted a stiff price for the troops he provided to win back Humayun's empire: unless Humayun "and all his adherents would become Shiites, he would make a funeral pile."[1] Humayun acceded reluctantly and, as a sign of agreement, donned the conical red turban of the Safavids. This caused resentment and discord in later years when orthodox Sunnis dominated the Mughal court.

With Persian help, Humayun recovered Kandahar and Kabul from his rebellious brothers; from these northern provinces he planned his recapture of the plains. Humayun was an odd and rather weak personality who grew increasingly superstitious and dependent upon opium. As his fortunes rose, his capacity declined, and it was his able general, Biram Khan, who routed the enemy in a soggy battle in the monsoon to recapture Hindustan. After fifteen years in exile, Humayun was enthroned in Delhi in July 1555. Scarcely six months later, he died as the result of a fall.

Few examples of architecture from Humayun's reign are known. Immediately after succeeding Babur, he had ordered construction of a handsome mosque in one of Babur's gardens opposite Agra. Today the stone has been quarried off and used for a village which has been built up around the shell of the mosque. Humayun is credited with designing a strange floating construction of barges joined together to form an octagon. He also built a bazaar on boats employing a similar construction and, "In like manner the royal gardeners made, in accordance with orders, a garden on the river."[2]

Humayun's most ambitious project was a new city which he called Dinpanah or World Refuge. The site he chose, on the banks of the holy Jumna near Delhi, was thought to be that of the legendary city of Indraprastha from the *Mahabharata*. The vast project was hastily begun in 1533 with a festive cornerstone-laying ceremony at which each of the nobles cemented a brick in place. No details, however, of the layout are known. During Humayun's exile, his city was razed and the Purana Qila, a new citadel, was constructed by Sher Shah.[3]

Located near the river beyond his unfinished city is Humayun's tomb. Begun in 1564, eight years after his death, it took nine years to complete. The tomb was sponsored by his widow, Haji Begum, and is believed to have been designed by a Persian, Mirak Mirza Ghiyas. While work was in progress, Haji Begum led a pilgrimage of royal women on her second journey to Mecca. According to legend, she brought back 200 Persian stonemasons to work on the tomb. However, this seems unlikely for the best stonemasons were Indian and the finely jointed stonework in the construction is clearly Indian. Babur had particularly admired the stonemasons, and had 680 men engaged on his Agra buildings alone.

Enclosures for tombs were not unknown in India, and two of the most unusual were island tombs of previous rulers of Delhi. The older is the austere fortified tomb of Ghiyas-ud-Din Tughluq built in the fourteenth century. The other was Sher Shah's sandstone mausoleum at Sasaram. The octagonal tomb of Sikandra Lodi, built in the Lodi necropolis in Delhi in 1517–1518, has a very low double dome and a walled enclosure.

The concept of setting monumental tombs within a large enclosed charbagh, however, was the Mughals' major contribution to garden architecture. The designs of tomb and garden were treated as one; the setting enhanced the beauty of the monument. Symbolically, it was far more—as the perfect embodiment of the ancient ideal, it was the ultimate Paradise Garden.

The large square enclosure, divided with geometric precision, was the ordered universe; in the center, the tomb itself rose like the cosmic mountain above the four rivers which were represented by the waterchannels. In the perpetual growing

Sasaram. Sher Shah's tomb. The walls of the large square courtyard rise dramatically from the water of the 1,000-foot tank surrounding the tomb. (Archaeological Survey of India)

season of Hindustan, there were eternal flowers and fruit, water and the perfume of Paradise.

The atmosphere lacked the seductive quality of the terraced pleasure gardens or the residential charbaghs of the emperors. Peaceful and harmonious, the tomb gardens suggested repose beyond earthly grief. Such great tombs, monuments honoring the dead, took on an almost religious quality; indeed, they were tended by a religious community and became pilgrimage sites.

The cosmic mountain was an ancient image long connected with the watercourses in the gardens and particularly favored by the Central Asians. The symbolism of the tomb, as the cosmic mountain, would have a strong appeal for someone like Humayun, who frequently consulted symbols as he became increasingly superstitious.[4]

His tomb garden in Delhi was the first such charbagh known. Extensively rebuilt and sensitively restored, it is the earliest Mughal garden in India with its original layout unchanged.

The garden covers approximately thirty acres, and is enclosed within high rough stone walls 360 meters long, each broken in the center by tall plastered gateways. From these gates, the garden is divided into quarters by gravel walks about forty feet wide; these lead to the tomb in the center. The plots are quartered repeatedly by narrower walks to form thirty-two plots in all.

Water enters the garden by a chevron-patterned chaddar in the northern gate. A large tank behind this gate, now filled from a drilled well, was originally filled from the Jumna. The river's course has changed, and it is now some distance from the garden. Narrow watercourses of cut limestone, fourteen inches wide and a few inches deep, run down the center of the main walks. These are

112

Delhi. Humayun's tomb.

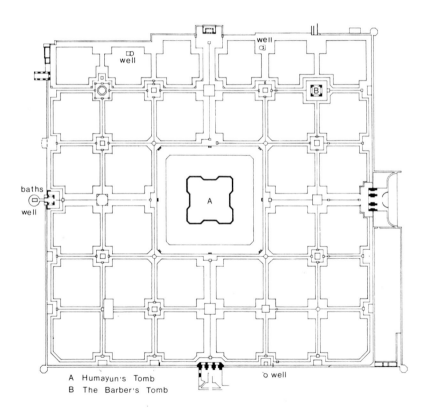

A Humayun's Tomb
B The Barber's Tomb

Late nineteenth-century reconstruction of Humayun's tomb. (Archeological Survey of India)

Delhi. Octagonal pool at corner of tomb and watercourse running across the garden.

intersected midway by square limestone pools; the narrowness of the channel encircling the tomb is emphasized at each corner by an octagonal pool. In keeping with the somber design, the pools and decoration are geometric—there is no foliation such as Babur used at Dholpur. The gravel walks with a curbing of undressed limestone are raised slightly above the planting beds. Clay pipes from the central waterchannel pass under them to irrigate the plots.

The tomb is set in the center of a broad, arcaded red sandstone terrace; both are decorated with white marble inlay. Four high iwan-like portals support the drum and graceful white marble shell of the outer dome.

Mughal tomb gardens were entered through a large forecourt. The gateway provided living quarters for the religious staff and the caretakers. The fruit from the garden and extensive orchard of this forecourt provided income for the maintenance of the tomb. Today, the watercourses at Humayun's tomb are dry, and the fruit trees have been replaced by grassy plots. A dignified atmosphere prevails in the vast, flat, open space.

ELEVEN

Akbar: Empire

In addition to political turmoil, the first years of Akbar's reign (1556–1605), were a dreadful period of drought, famine, and epidemic in India. However, the rich court life did not diminish during these disasters; whenever one occurred, the Mughals did very little to relieve the suffering of the population.

Only thirteen years old when crowned, the boy-emperor, Akbar, was at first interested only in sport and the army; affairs of state were left to his guardian. When he assumed control a few years later, however, he stood independent of close advisors and so remained throughout his long reign. He first asserted himself by abolishing the tax on Indian pilgrims and a tax on non-Muslims. This was unpopular with his Sunni-dominated court, but popular with the public. Akbar is well-remembered to this day in India.

He had great intellectual curiosity, an amazing memory, and was a learned man though he had neither the interest nor the patience required to learn to read and write. Manuscripts were read to him by men chosen for their pleasant voices. The *Babur-Nama* was a favorite, and he referred to it as "The Memoirs of Babur, the Conqueror of the World, which may be called a Code to Practical Wisdom."[1]

A man of exceptional physical strength, energy and bravery, Akbar often led his own troops. His desire for conquest was never satisfied, and he expanded the empire throughout his reign. He built continuously and firmly established the Imperial Mughal style of architecture. His projects reflected his ambitions and were usually large, stone fortresses in key cities of strategic states. The small palace in one such fort, at Ajmer, is today a museum. Akbar ordered his officers and nobles "to build suitable houses and gardens surrounding it."[2] As the emperor directed, so the court acted! Most of these houses and the fort itself have disappeared although some of Akbar's exceptionally high fort walls today weave through the crowded city. Years later, Jahangir built a large charbagh along the shore of the lake at Ajmer; both he and Shah Jahan embellished it with a series of lakeside marble pavilions. In December 1819, Lt. Colonel James Tod, the political agent to the western Rajput states, visited Ajmer and found the

Ajmer. Arches from pavilion along lake front terrace of gardens.

gardens pleasant "but the imperial residence of marble ... now going fast to decay. The walks on which his majesty last paraded, in the state-coach sent by our James the First, are now overgrown with shrubs."[3] Little of this royal complex stands today. A pleasant public garden on the site of Jahangir's charbagh has some large old shade trees, but no Mughal character. A marble esplanade extends along the shore line; on it two graceful, small pavilions and a row of ghostly arches testify to the beauty of the long gone palace. Ajmer is one of the most attractive natural settings of any Mughal site.

The love of gardens that Babur's chieftains brought with them to the plains of Hindustan remained strong in their descendants. Akbar's finance advisor, the brilliant Ja'far Beg, was reputed to be a skilled gardener who not only pruned his own garden, but planted it as well. So passionate a gardener was he that often he transacted business while working in his garden. Although his interest in gardens was limited, Akbar was said to have built a Paradise Garden beyond Agra. It had disappeared by the beginning of Jahangir's reign in 1605.

While constructing his largest and most splendid fort at Agra, Akbar built an entirely new city a day's journey away, and named it Fathepur Sikri. Babur had built a large garden near the village of Sikri, sixty miles northeast of his Dholpur garden along the same sandstone ridge. To build his city, Akbar had the stone quarried on the spot from this great ridge.

The work required hundreds of stonemasons from other parts of the realm, resulting in a rich mix of regional styles in the wonderful stonework. The compact palace buildings, set on a series of broad stone terraces, had aqueducts built into their construction. Some of the intricate, clever waterworks remain.

Fathepur Sikri became known as a cultural center where the emperor led discussions on theology with learned men of all creeds, including European Christian missionaries. A discerning patron, he enjoyed painting and had a brilliant atelier. The splendid miniatures of this period richly detail court life.

Akbar created a new, though poorly defined, religion which centered on the person of the king—indeed, he declared the king divine. His concept of kingship is manifested in his odd throne in the Diwan-i Khas, or hall of private audience, at Fathepur Sikri. A single, richly decorated, octagonal pillar rises fifteen feet in the center of the small room. From it, a series of intricately carved brackets extend like the branches of a tree and support a circular platform for the king. From this regal perch, four narrow stone walks radiate to the corners of the building. This odd tree of state revives the old concept of the cosmic tree.

There are no traces or descriptions of the imperial gardens which stretched between the royal buildings and the lakefront, nor of the rich commercial city which sprang up below the palaces. Shortly before it was abandoned, the estimated population of Fathepur Sikri was 200,000. Thousands of people were required at court for entertainment and sport alone: 1,000 swordsmen and wrestlers, hundreds of musicians, dancers and poets; scores of men to train birds and animals in every type of competition from hawking to frog-fighting.

Although Akbar raised a few unusually gifted and effective Hindus to high positions in his court, most of his nobles and officers were Muslim descendants of foreign invaders. They were joined by Persian immigrants seeking their fortunes in the splendid and expanding court of the Great Mughal.

Fathepur Sikri. Section showing aqueduct incorporated into structure.

Bari. Partial view of double line of chhatris along bund. Pavilions of sunken garden to the left; deserted walled garden in the distance.

Autocratic and unpredictable, Akbar was fascinated by administration and maintained strong central control over his empire. The administrative structure he created and which continued for the duration of the dynasty was essentially military, so a noble's title was military—though he might be a poet or the keeper of the royal seals. Thus Dost Muhammad, the engineer who laid out Jahangir's gardens at Agra and the Fort at Lahore, was given the honorary title: Khwajah Jahan, commander of 4,000. A commander's salary and allowance from the Crown increased as the number of standing troops he maintained increased. Such men supported a large staff and household, and spent vast sums on the excessive display necessary to maintain a position at court.

On his death, a noble's possessions and wealth went to the Crown. An allowance was made to the family and, with influence at court, a command might be secured for a son. It was not difficult to acquire wealth but it was hard to pass it on. This system, in which security and success depended on the emperor's pleasure, encouraged spending and corruption by the nobles. It also explains much of the building by members of the Mughal court. Royal favor was sought by catering to the emperor's whims and appealing to his vanity. When Jahangir laid out royal gardens, dozens of nobles followed his example and built lavish charbaghs; as he was fond of roses, there was a vogue for rose gardens during his reign. In the early years of his reign, Shah Jahan began the Taj Mahal, a tomb for his wife, Mumtaz Mahal, planned on an unprecedented scale. He spent much time selecting the design and decorated it with precious stones; by example he encouraged his nobles to build tombs. Many of these tombs remain, decaying

118

Sikandra. Painting of Akbar's tomb. Inaccurate but charming. Note gardener at work.
(Private collection)

and somewhat romantic ruins amidst the teeming bustle and tumble of Indian city life, their gardens long since taken over for some urban use.

One picturesque example of such court behavior is Khanpur Mahal, a remote palace with deserted gardens several miles beyond Dholpur. The approach is along a wide bund, or earthen dam, above a man-made lake. Two rows of octagonal sandstone chhatris, with the deep bracketed eaves and engrailed arches favored by Shah Jahan, line the bund.

The lake is unusually blue and, like all the waters of Central India, attracts a wonderful variety of water birds. Giant cranes from beyond the Himalayas soar above it, and small birds cluster in colorful clouds on its vivid surface. Handsome, brilliant red sandstone buildings along the shore between the bund and a forest are reflected in the water; one of the most charming sites of the Mughal era.

Originally the lower side of the bund must have been lined with a series of gardens; today there are remains of only one. An unusual, small walled garden, it is entered by a narrow stairway which leads down through the bund and gives it the feeling of a sunken garden. Twin pavilions face each other across a shallow area which apparently once held water devices. Indeed, the decaying garden appears to have been a water garden. At the far end of the bund is a mysterious walled garden, locked and deserted.

Locally it is said the Khanpur Mahal was built in expectation of a visit from Shah Jahan by his local provincial official (ca. 1640). The emperor never arrived, hence the palace remained unoccupied. It stood empty for over a hundred years, and is today used by the Rajasthan State Government.

Though earlier Timurids had briefly controlled Kashmir, in 1588 Akbar decisively conquered the valley. He cut a road through the tortuous mountain passes and opened the valley to development by his descendants. He brought 200 Indian master builders to Kashmir to quarry the limestone in the valley and build a fort in the Imperial Mughal manner. Though he completed a lakeside garden, he never finished his hilltop citadel overlooking Dal Lake.

Having firmly established the Mughal Empire, on his deathbed Akbar bestowed his Imperial turban and Humayun's sword on his oldest son, the new emperor, Jahangir. Thus ended forty-nine years of absolute—and brilliant—rule. In writing about Akbar's burial, which he found surprisingly simple, a Jesuit missionary observed, "Thus does the world treat those from whom no good is to be hoped, nor evil feared."[4]

TWELVE

Jahangir: Pleasure

The valley of Kashmir, protected from influence, as well as invasion by its circle of thickly wooded mountains, had developed its own architectural tradition. Stone temples had been built during the ancient Buddhist and Hindu periods, but in later centuries the buildings were of wood. They were square and multi-storied with distinctive, pyramidal roofs covered with turf. In the spring tiny iris and tulips, planted in the turf to hold it in place, turned these rooftops into gardens. On his visits to Kashmir, Jahangir made special trips around the valley to see these most beautiful rooftops.

Attracted by the splendor of the mountains and the charm of the lakes and streams, Jahangir made the hazardous journey to Kashmir often. His colorful descriptions of it are the least restrained in his Memoirs: "If one were to take to praise Kashmir, whole books would have to be written."[1] He observed and noted everything and found the watermelons and pears of the best kind, the garlic good, much admired the soft wool shawls, and declared the plumes of feathers among "its excellencies." He rated the fish inferior and the wine sour. He disliked the rice and thought the grain poor; the pomegranates not worth much, the guavas middling—but the apricots could rival Kabul's.

Jahangir found Akbar's garden within the citadel sadly neglected and ordered it rebuilt. He was delighted by its appearance when completed:

> The lake is close to the fort, and the palace overlooks the water. In the palace there was a little garden, with a small building in it in which my revered father used constantly to sit. At this period it appeared to me to be very much out of order and ruinous .... I ordered Mu'tamid K., who is a servant who knows my temperment to make every effort to put the little garden in order and repair the buildings. In a short space of time, through his great assiduity, it acquired new beauty. In the garden he put up a lofty terrace 32 yards square, in three divisions, and having repaired the building he adorned it with pictures by masterhands, and so made it the envy of the picture gallery of China. I called this garden Nur-afza (light increasing.)[2]

Srinigar, Kashmir. Abandoned, stone Mughal building with damaged lotus finial. Situated at Hari Pabat, the fort above the city and the lake.

According to Jahangir, cherry and apricot trees were brought to Kashmir from Kabul by Akbar. Not unexpectedly, when he rebuilt Akbar's fort garden he included cherry trees. When four of these trees produced a crop of 1,500 delicious cherries, he gave them whimsical names and "strictly ordered the officials of Kashmir to plant shah-alu (cherry) trees in all the gardens."[3]

In the cool altitude of Kashmir, 5,200 feet, apples and plums were substituted for the usual orange and citron trees bordering the paths. White, purple, and mauve iris were a favorite floral combination and lilac the favorite shrub.

As Akbar had before him, Jahangir took an interest in the economically important crop of saffron which he estimated to be about 25,000 pounds. Of its cultivation he wrote, "the land is not ploughed or irrigated, the plant springs up amongst the clods."[4] Another year he visited the fields during the harvest and found "groves on groves, and plains on plains were in bloom. The breeze in that place scented one's brain. The stem is attached to the ground. The flower has four petals, and its colour is that of a violet. It is the size of a champa flower, and from the middle of it three stigmas of saffron grow .... The custom is for half to go to the government and half to the cultivators ... they take half its weight in salt as wages. There is no salt in Kashmir, and they bring it from Hindustan."[5]

Jahangir continually rhapsodized about the valley: "Kashmir is a garden of eternal spring...a delightful flower-bed, and a heart-expanding heritage for dervishes. Its pleasant meads and enchanting cascades are beyond all description. There are running streams and fountains beyond count. Wherever the eye reaches, there are verdure and running water."[6]

The emperor commissioned a collection of paintings of Kashmiri wildflowers by one of his favorite painters: "The flowers that are seen in the territories of Kashmir are beyond all calculation. Those that Nadiru-l-asri Ustad Mansur has painted are more than 100."[7] Milo C. Beach has described the natural history paintings of Mansur as achieving the "perfect balance of naturalistic and formal concerns—and are thereby typical of the Jahangiri style."[8]

This period marks the development of portraiture and individuality in Mughal paintings which, Professor Beach maintains, "show a close observation of the technical and intellectual bases of available European works." During Jahangir's reign, there were frequent Western visitors to the Mughal court who presented European paintings to the emperor. It is quite possible that the emperor's fondness for his gardens inspired them to present him with some of the garden literature and herbals beginning to be produced in Europe, or even prints of European gardens. In contrast to the paintings, however, there is no European influence evident in the design of Jahangir's gardens. Apparently the European designs did not suit the emperor's taste nor did Mughal garden designers feel the need to import ideas. With his knowledge of plants and interest in their use, Jahangir's geometric charbaghs were that "pefect balance of naturalistic and formal concerns," unlike the more rigidly formal European gardens, and they served a different purpose.

Increasingly in Europe in the seventeenth century, gardens symbolized the monarch's power, a trend which climaxed in the 1660s in the ever-expanding gardens of Versailles. In discussing how the "growth of the King's power can be charted by the growing number of acres added to the gardens and parks," Howard Adams has written: "The sequence of the development of the gardens at Versailles is intimately related to the emerging power of the King, his concept of the monarchy, and his love affairs. All three influences were at times entangled in the expansion and use of the gardens to further the King's policies or to celebrate an amorous conquest."[9]

The power of the Mughal emperor was absolute and increasingly manifest by his expanding court, lavish dress, and opulent court life and palaces. However, because of the age-old mystical response aroused by the Paradise gardens they were not perceived of as displays of power, but rather intended to be places of perfect peace.

On their visits to Kashmir, the emperors usually resided in the royal apartments of Akbar's fort, Hari Parbat, and visited the pleasure gardens by *shikara*, or Kashmiri boats. In the first half of the seventeenth century, the Vale of Kashmir was reputed to have 777 gardens dotting the lakesides and mountain slopes, all built by Jahangir, his son Shah Jahan, and their nobles. As much as they admired the wooden Kashmiri buildings with their turf roofs, they did not adopt the style and continued to build flat-roofed pavilions of stone.[10]

In March 1665, François Bernier, a French physician who spent six years in the Mughal empire, accompanied Jahangir's grandson, the Emperor Aurengzeb, to Kashmir. He observed: "The lake is full of islands, which are so many pleasure

Shah Jahan seated on a terrace in a garden in Kashmir. Note stepping stones across channel above cascade. Ca. 1642. (Copyright The British Library)

grounds. They look beautiful and green in the midst of the water, being covered with fruit trees, and laid out with regular trellised walks. In general they are surrounded by the large-leafed aspen, planted at intervals of two feet. The largest of these trees may be clasped in a man's arms, but they are as high as the mast of a ship, and have only a tuft of branches at the top, like the palm trees.

"The declivities of the mountains beyond the lake are crowded with houses and flower-gardens. The air is healthful, and the situation considered most desirable: they abound with springs and streams of water, and command a delightful view of the lake, the islands, and the town."[11]

Unlike the gardens of the plains where small amounts of water were used with great effect, the abundance of water in the valley of Kashmir inspired its gardens. Water tumbled down the chaddars, cascaded into imaginative waterfalls, and churned into the ample pools. Glittering water surrounded and flowed under and through the buildings. Fountains played continuously in the canals and pools, the whitened spray carried on the gentle mountain breezes. The customary narrow watercourses were widened to shallow canals interrupted by stepping stones. The emperor's throne was often built across the canals above a cascade and seemed to float on the water. The lush world outside the gardens was dominated by the sight and sound of water, rivers, springs, lakes, and rice paddies. The entire valley was silver and green.

In this century, scarcity of water has become a problem in Kashmir. The severe deforestation of the mountains has resulted in serious erosion and a drop in the water table, and the annual snowfall and amount of rainfall has decreased. Water is being conserved for more vital uses than ornamental gardens. Along the lakeside only a very few Mughal charbaghs remain today and these survive in greatly altered condition and without flowing water. These gardens have not been restored; rather, they have been repaired and modernized and currently serve as parks. Without water these gardens are robbed of their original character. Pleasant as they may be, all semblance to the atmosphere of the old Paradise gardens has been lost.

Shalimar, a garden conceived of by Jahangir and perfected by Shah Jahan, was once the most fabled garden in the world. Bernier thought it the most beautiful of all the gardens and described the approach by shikara: "The entrance from the lake is through a spacious canal, bordered with green turf, and running between two rows of poplars. Its length is about five hundred paces, and it leads to a large summerhouse placed in the middle of the garden." [12]

Bewitched by the spell of the water at Shalimar, the Vicomte Robert d'Humieres, the French traveler, described an evening in the garden at the turn of the century in: "a kiosk with black marble columns, in the middle of a square bason. From three sides of the square fell three cascades, whose sheet of mobile crystal was illumined by lamps set behind them in recesses. The fourth side opened out the perspective of a long canal bordered with lights, with a line of playing waters as

Kashmir. Shalimar. "Black Pavilion" with heavy pipes in surrounding pool. The stone pillars are the original Mughal. Wooden roof is a much later addition.

Kashmir. Nishat Bagh. View from upper terrace down central watercourse. Original approach by boat was through the narrow gate cut in the bund across the lake in the background.

an axis, the last of which ran out towards the lake in moonlit distances. Four other rows of spouting fountains in the bason itself raised as it were a forest of silver lances around the kiosk with its glittering marbles. We were surrounded by the splashing, by the efficient coolness of the heavenly water, the glory of the consoling water, the feast and the apotheosis of water." [13]

Today water flows in Shalimar briefly in the spring, and in other seasons only once a week for a few hours. The lovely black stone pavilion still stands but with a peaked wooden roof. Its tank is dry and cluttered with heavy iron pipes and floodlights for a "son et lumiere." Portions of walls between two terraces have been demolished to provide space for seating.

As in the other surviving charbaghs, the side plots of the terraces are planted with lawns occasionally interspersed with flower beds, while other flower beds border the pathways where avenues of gay fruit trees once shaded them. These flower beds are similar to those popular in Europe in the nineteenth century—serpentine or irregularly shaped with low bedding plants. Picturesque wooden buildings sit on the stone platforms of the elegant Mughal pavilions. In most of the charbaghs the terracing and dry central watercourse are the only authentic remainders of Mughal design.[14]

The Mughals had a genius for siting their gardens. In some instances in Kashmir, it can be seen that the configuration of the mountains above the garden adds drama to the site. Often they would pipe water or divert rivers to a stunning site, rather than have the garden built at the site of the water. Perhaps the most dramatic site was chosen by Dara Shukoh, Shah Jahan's favorite son, 600 feet above the lake on the jutting vertical edge of a mountain. Built for his teacher, an astrologer revered as a holy man, it consisted of seven terraces representing the planets. Water was piped from a spring a kilometer away to the central watercourse. From the garden, there is a misty view of the valley, about twenty miles wide, with Akbar's fort crowning a hill across the lake.

Communication with the fort and other gardens from this lovely aerie was by pigeon, and an unusual two-story pigeon house is the largest structure in the complex. All the buildings were of rough limestone blocks and originally had plastered walls. The pigeon house extends from the center of the supporting wall of the fifth terrace and is approached along a handsome gallery.

The garden was built in 1640, and was used for only fifty years before being abandoned. It was called Pari Mahal, or Fairy House, by the local people, who were afraid to visit the site because they believed it to be haunted and because they feared snakes on the mountainside.

Kashmir. Pari Mahal. The pigeon house from the terrace below.

Restoration of Pari Mahal is under way, but the completed terrace is planted in a modern design without Mughal influence. Stiff beds of roses extend across the old watercourse and there is neither water nor trees.

The ruin of Pari Mahal is romantically outlined against the sky from the garden of Chasma Shahi, a small garden built in 1632–1633. In the main pavilion, there is a rare treatment of water: beneath the open watercourse, which flows through the pavilion, runs a second channel. Water from the top channel flows into a five-foot-square pool and some returns through the lower, hidden channel to the main watercourse; thus it recirculates. The overflow from the pool descends to the lower terrace by an exceptionally long, about eighteen feet, but narrow chaddar.

There are still some magnificent chenars in the gardens, for it is a protected tree in Kashmir. Its beautiful leaf is the most common design on Kashmiri textiles and handicrafts. The tree was brought to Kashmir by the Mughals, and there was one spectacular Mughal grove of 300 chenars in symmetrical rows. Of another chenar grove Jahangir wrote: "About a hundred plane-trees of graceful form clustered together on one plot of ground, pleasant and green, join each other so as to shade the whole plot, and the whole surface of the ground is grass and trefoil; so much so that to lay a carpet on it would be superfluous and in bad taste." [15]

Beautiful old chenars still shade Achbal, a remote garden built by Jahangir at the southern end of the valley. The water gushes from a spring with such force and cascades into the pools with such power that it creates a very lively atmosphere in the garden. Originally, an underground channel was necessary to carry off the excess water; today much of it is used for a trout hatchery which adjoins the garden. In Achbal the water changes character on the same plane by moving from pool to canal to pool; the usual design is varied because the pools are longer than the connecting watercourse.

Jahangir called Kashmir "Paradise on Earth" and wished to be buried there in his favorite garden at Vernag, on the approach to the Banihal Pass. A steep mountain rises sharply behind the great spring, an ancient place of worship for Kashmiris—for centuries it was known as Nila Naga, a holy spring for a snake cult. Jahangir ordered a palace and gardens laid out around an octagonal pool built about the spring. Today, but for the twenty-four arched recesses surrounding the pool at the water level, his buildings have disappeared. A twelve-foot-wide canal runs almost a thousand feet from the pool to the river Bihat. The atmosphere is peaceful but pagan, reminiscent of a shrine to a water deity.

On the arduous journey south before the autumn storms, Jahangir died in the mountains beyond Kashmir. His wish to be buried at Vernag was unfulfilled for his body was taken to Lahore and buried in an old garden rebuilt by his queen, Nur Jahan, which she renamed Shahdara. As at other Mughal tomb sites and still in existence at Shahdara, the forecourt was built as a serai with deep alcoves on a terrace in the encircling wall. In this enclosure, a narrow channel running along the edge of the terrace watered the groves of fruit trees planted in the plots. The flow of water was regulated by the customary barrages, and it simply fell to the garden about four feet below.

A self-indulgent man, Jahangir's interest in sport and nature had been keener than his interest in governing. An avid hunter, he cared more for the kill than for expanding the kingdom so his reign was marked by relative peace. He continued the administrative practices of Akbar, and to implement them he relied on the father and the brother of his queen, Nur Jahan.

An enthusiastic patron of painting, Jahangir also wrote his *Memoirs*. They reveal his surprising insight into the character of those around him, portraying him as capable but disinterested. His weakness was the family addiction to drugs and alcohol; as these weakened him he relied increasingly upon Nur Jahan. Little wonder that a controversy arose over the active role assumed by the queen. While it was not unusual for women to influence affairs, Nur Jahan's intelligence and energy prompted her to seek a greater role. On the death of her father, the prime minister, Jahangir bestowed "everything belonging to the government and Amirship of Itimad-ud daulah to Nur Jahan Begam."[16] During a prolonged illness for the last five years of Jahangir's life, Nur Jahan was the virtual ruler of India.

When her adversary, Shah Jahan, succeeded in the struggle for the throne following Jahangir's death, Nur Jahan retired to a life of seclusion in Lahore. She survived Jahangir by eighteen years which she spent overseeing completion of Shahdara and construction of her own tomb. In Agra, Nur Jahan had built the tomb of her father, Itimad-ud Daulah, the first example in India of marble inlaid with semi-precious stones; she used subtle variations of earth tones in floral and geometric patterns. Her own tomb has been described as quite similar and, like his, was set back on a square plinth. Water dropped into the waterchannels dividing the charbagh from pools set in each side of the platform. The charbagh was said to be 400 yards square and contained the small palace where she lived. Nur Jahan's mausoleum barely survives today; stripped of its decoration, it is a mournful ruin, and the limits of its garden cannot even be traced.

Agra. Tomb of Itimad-ud Daulah, 1628.
Detail of marble inlay in pattern of cypress
and fruit trees.

THIRTEEN

Shah Jahan: Decline

Shah Jahan enjoyed a reputation as an efficient monarch and from 1627 to 1657 presided over one of the most lavish courts the world had seen. However, it was his seizure of the throne which marked the beginning of the decline of the Mughals: he violated the strict Timurid tradition of sanctuary for princes.

Even the ruthless Timur had honored family ties; when his code was broken by his descendants, evil fortune and often death overtook them.[1] On his deathbed, Babur had admonished Humayun, "Do naught against your brothers, even though they may deserve it."[2] Though his brothers dealt with him treacherously, he forgave them; even they observed the code. On his desperate flight to Persia, pursued by his brother Askari, Humayun was forced to leave the infant Akbar behind. Askari captured Akbar and gave him sanctuary and devoted care.

The strongest and most competent of Jahangir's sons, Shah Jahan was the favorite. Although the third son, born of the Rajput princess who was Jahangir's first wife, Shah Jahan was apparently Jahangir's chosen successor until a strain developed between them during the emperor's declining years. Nur Jahan, Jahangir's beloved and powerful Persian queen, bore him no children, but intrigued against Shah Jahan in favor of his younger brother. When forced into open defiance against his father, Shah Jahan was forced to leave two of his young sons at court as hostages. Knowing the time-honored Timurid tradition, he could continue his rebellious behavior confident of their safety. Already suspected of the murder of his elder brother, at Jahangir's death Shah Jahan ordered the murder of that brother's son. To secure the throne he had his younger brother and two cousins killed.

Shah Jahan ended his life virtually a prisoner of his son Aurangzeb, having witnessed deception and fratricide among his sons in their battle for succession. Once he broke the fundamental principle of Timurid rule and weakened the bonds of blood, Shah Jahan fatally weakened the empire.

In spite of his ambition and extreme selfishness, Shah Jahan appears to have been fond of his children, and his devotion to his queen is legendary. He called her Mumtaz Mahal, "Light of the World," and insisted she accompany him on all of his military campaigns. A few years after he began his rule, she died while giving birth to her fifteenth child on a campaign in the Deccan. Shah Jahan built the Taj Mahal as her tomb and intended that it be the most splendid building in the world.

The Taj Mahal is an unforgettable visual experience. With every change of light there appear subtle variations in the hue of the luminous marble; at times it appears to be a vision. Constructed and decorated of costly materials, yet the tomb is strikingly simple. Indeed it is the embodiment of perfection: architectur-ally, in its balance, symmetry and proportion; and visually, in its apparent suspension between earth and sky.[3] The graceful structure with its slightly swelling dome is framed by four tapering minarets. Its elegant pinnacle is adapted from the finial of the Hindu temple; a spire rises from a lotus blossom, it holds a Hindu water pot and at the top, a lotus bud.[4]

For many years speculation has existed about the accuracy of a legend that Shah Jahan intended to build his own tomb of black marble in the same design within a garden across the river. However appealing such a romantic legend may be, contemporary histories and examination of Mughal construction on the opposite bank do not support the theory.

The Mehtab Bagh which once existed here was part of "Kabul," the long series of charbaghs built by Babur and his Begs on the east bank of the Jumna. It is now farmland, and several stone chabutras, simple sandstone platforms, almost buried by crops, are the only relics of the buildings in fields where bullocks still raise water from the old Mughal wells. The remaining riverfront pavilions are inferior in size and simpler in design to those of Shah Jahan's in the Taj enclosure. There is neither heavy reinforcing of the wall which would be necessary to support a building of any size, nor massive substructure comparable to the construction of the waterfront terrace of the Taj.[5]

Within its enclosure, the first sight of the Taj Mahal at the end of the long watercourse, seeming as it does to float above its marble plinth, has a powerful emotional appeal. Set on a riverfront terrace above the end of the charbagh, its placement is a departure from the usual tradition where the monument is placed in the center of a charbagh.

However, the tomb once stood between two charbaghs, separated by the river.

Viewed from the opposite riverfront pavilion, the Taj is mirrored in the river: an earthly tomb floating toward the heavens, an ethereal tomb floating on the sacred waters. The tomb and its image united the two charbaghs, and it is thus in the center of an ordered universe—the Paradise ideal.

That the identification of the Taj enclosure with Paradise was intended seems clear from the selection of the inscription on the south gate, the main entrance to the garden. The quotation, from the Koran, is the chapter known as "The Daybreak" which ends with an invitation to the reader to enter Paradise.[6]

The meticulous planning of the tomb complex includes the details of the charbagh itself. The pressure system of the fountains and the waterworks which supplied them are the most unusual features of the Taj charbagh. To insure even distribution and equal water pressure in the fountains, copper pots were inserted between the underground water pipes and the fountains in the watercourse.[7] Not until water filled all the pots did it rise to the fountains. The fountains—marble

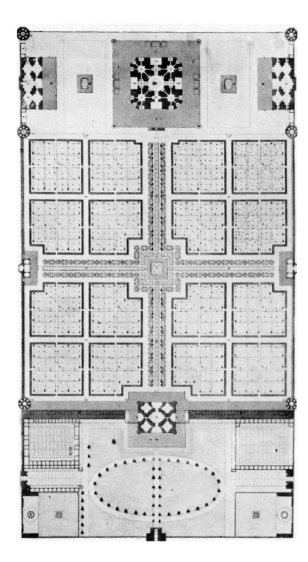

Agra. Plan of tomb and garden of the Taj Mahal. The garden itself is 800 feet wide, and 975 feet from the gate to the tomb. (Archaeological Survey of India drawing by J. H. Hodgson (1828), then Surveyor General of India)

lotus buds—were only placed in the main water channel and not in the cross channel. In the center of the garden, the raised, square, foliated pool has five fountains.

The water supply for the garden came from the Jumna and was stored in a massive tank outside the west gate of the Taj enclosure. *Purs*, or a rope and buckets, hauled by bullocks treading a huge ramp, raised the water from the river into a high aqueduct which fed the storage tank.

Professor R. Nath, who has made a study of the Taj, has suggested that the architect of the garden originally intended the view of the monument from the south gate to be unobstructed by plants or trees in the garden. He found that the original irrigation system provided an adequate supply of water near the main channel and very little to the sections farthest from the main waterchannel. He interprets this to mean that trees were planted in the further plots and flowers and low shrubs near the channel between the entrance gates and the tomb.[8]

During the last years of his life when he was confined to his quarters in the Red Fort at Agra, Shah Jahan had a splendid view down the river of the Taj Mahal shimmering in the distance.

As a young prince, Shah Jahan had been close to his grandfather, the Great Akbar. Like him, he built a new city; glorifying himself, he called it Shahjahanabad. The astonishing, new cities of Fathepur Sikri and Shahjahanabad were built to please one person—the absolute ruler of a vast empire who was not intimidated or influenced by the taste of others.

Today, Akbar's abandoned Fathepur Sikri is maintained by the Archaeological Survey of India, and only a few watchmen tread its stone passages after sunset. In contrast, the two square miles of the walled city of Shahjahanabad, commonly known as Old Delhi, are a thriving commercial and industrial center. Shah

Plan of water-supply system for Taj. Taken from Hodgson's plan. (Archaeological Survey of India)

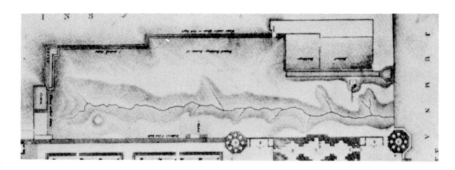

Section of water-supply system of Taj Mahal. Water is raised from the level of the river through three sets of purs to large, raised storage tanks outside the west wall.

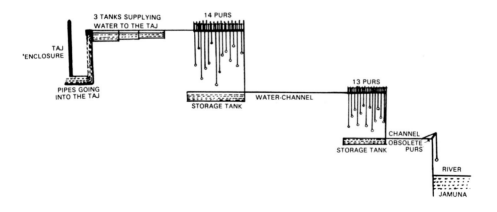

Emperor Muhammad Shah in his Garden, *ca.* 1735. The elegant garden near Delhi is similar to the Red Fort. It is shown in great detail, and includes an arbor extending to each side of the pavilion. (Courtesy, Museum of Fine Arts, Boston)

Jahan's great mosque, the Jama Masjid, soars amid a maze of alleys and streets teeming with some three quarters of a million people. The moat and gardens which formerly lay between the city and the stern walls of the Red Fort are gone. Once the royal residence, most of the Fort is today occupied by the military.

The Fort was completed in 1648. Viewed about forty years later by François Bernier, the French doctor, the gardens along the moat were "filled at all times with flowers and green shrubs, which, contrasted with the stupendous red walls, produced a beautiful effect."[9]

Within the walls, the private apartments were composed of a series of white marble pavilions spaced irregularly along a 1,600-foot terrace and linked by a marble waterchannel. On one side these pavilions were open to formal gardens, and on the other, through exquisitely carved marble *jallis,* they overlooked the river, sixty feet below. Old paintings show them in their splendor: shaded by the brilliant scarlet silk awnings of the emperor, and with gilded cupolas on the gay chattris. Shah Jahan enjoyed musical evenings on this zenana terrace as the scent of sandalwood and rose water mingled with the perfume of the *Mahtab Bagh*, or Moonlight Garden. The Mughals had adopted the old Indian tradition of planting fragrant, white, night-flowering plants in their moon-drenched gardens. The daily cycle in India has not changed greatly since the Mughals. Then as now,

134

the day began with priests intoning prayers at dawn, while the cities were stirring and farmers were off to work in the fields.

Early morning was the loveliest time of day: heavy dew coated the grass and rimmed flowers like pearls, then rose in a moist and silvery haze. Midday was quiet as the scorching sun drove people to seek shade or remain indoors. In the evening, the Mughals enjoyed their Moonlight Gardens. When candlelight flickered in the niches of pavilion walls and the edges of platforms above the waterchannels, which reflected the moonlight, these charbaghs seemed most like Paradise.

The Mughals adopted several other Indian floral customs such as that of hanging a string of *asoka* or mango leaves above a doorway, an auspicious sign of welcome. The women of the zenana often decorated their hair with creamy champaka blossoms which have an overpowering scent, and wove necklaces of jasmine blossoms which they wore in the Indian fashion.

The witty French doctor, Bernier, wrote an amusing description of a visit he made to the private quarters within Shahjahanabad. It is probably the best contemporary description we are likely to find of this lovely purdah palace:

> Who is the traveller that can describe from ocular observation the interior of that building? I have sometimes gone into it when the King was absent from Delhi, and once pretty far I thought, for the purpose of giving my professional advice in the case of a great lady so extremely ill that she could not be moved to the outward gate, according to the customs observed upon similar occasions; but a Kachemire shawl covered my head, hanging like a large scarf down to my feet, and an eunuch led me by the hand, as if I had been a blind man. You must be content, therefore, with such a general description as I have received from some of the eunuchs. They inform me that the Seraglio contains beautiful apartments, separated, and more or less spacious and splendid, according to the rank and income of the females. Nearly every chamber has its reservoir of running water at the door; on every side are gardens, delightful alleys, shady retreats, streams, fountains, grottoes,[10] deep excavations that afford shelter from the sun by day, lofty divans and terraces, on which to sleep coolly at night. Within the walls of this enchanting place, in fine, no oppressive or inconvenient heat is felt.[11]

In 1828, when the Red Fort was inspected by Captain Robert Smith, he found the gardens in dilapidated condition: "The gardens, which are now a complete wilderness, being filled with rubbish and overgrown with weeds, still retain the traces of their early beauty and grandeur, although the waters of the basins and fountains are nearly dried up; many of these were of very beautiful mosaic; tho' now sadly disfigured, the most valuable parts having been picked out, and must have been, before the rude hand of the despoilers robbed them of their beauty, masterpieces indeed of art and taste."[12]

There has been much restoration and, unfortunately, some building. Within the fort today, ugly nineteenth-century barracks stand on the site of the Mahtab Bagh and loom over the restored riverside terrace. The airy pavilions of the private apartments, with bays of engrailed arches and wonderfully carved interiors, are beautiful—but it is a ravaged beauty, evocative of former glory, a reminder of a violent past. Without water, there is an almost sterile atmosphere in these once sensuous pavilions.

Delhi. Red Fort. Modern water tower behind marble pavilion supplies an army building and not the garden.

The *Hayat Baksh,* or life-bestowing garden, once had stately rows of cypress and beds of saffron, crimson and purple flowers, a favorite combination in the colorful Timurid charbaghs. Today the garden area is modernized with lawns and low, clipped hedges and flower beds, though it is still planted in the old colors. The gardens of the Red Fort, once the most splendid of Mughal Gardens, lack even the melancholy charm of a ruin.

His affection for Akbar did not deter him and in 1627, the year he seized the throne, Shah Jahan demolished some of Akbar's vigorously carved red sandstone buildings within the Agra fort and replaced them with marble palaces; others he had covered with marble plaster. This plaster, containing marble dust, has the appearance of the solid marble when it is highly polished. Little of Akbar's 500 buildings now remains within his great gates. In the courtyard of one splendid palace, the Jahangiri Mahal, a circular baoli from Akbar's era is in fine condition.[13]

Of those that remain, the best palace court garden is the Anguri Bagh, or grape garden, built by Shah Jahan of his favorite white marble in the Agra fort. The Khas Mahal, Shah Jahan's open pavilion with cusped Indian arches, was actually the highest story of a building with rooms on many levels constructed as part of the walls of the great fort. Forming the east side of the Anguri Bagh enclosure, the Khas Mahal was set far back on a wide marble platform bordered by a delicately carved, low marble balustrade. In the center, its foliated edge flush with the platform, was one of the loveliest of Mughal pools. The substance of the marble is like a scroll, and void of the water is an elegant trefoil design. The

136

Anguri Bagh at the turn of the century showing Khas Mahal and curbing in plots.
(Archaeological Survey of India)

Detail of curbing within the four plots.

Agra Fort. Detail of pool set in Khas Mahal terrace. Note similarity in design to Lotus
Garden, Dholpur.

corners are carved as lotus petals as in the lower pool in Babur's Lotus Garden. Fountain jets were embedded in the scrolls, and the five fountains in the pool had needle-like jets.

A shallow waterchannel ran from the pool to the edge of the platform, designed in a striking chevron pattern of marble inlay in pale shades of green and red with white separated by narrow bands of black. The water fell vertically into a five-foot oval tub on the garden level. As it fell, it cascaded in front of a marble slab with three rows of five niches, or decorative pigeon holes.

According to Dr. Saifur Rahman Dar, these decorative niches were first introduced into gardens during Akbar's time by Jahangir's future father-in-law in his garden in Lahore.[14] The gracefully carved recesses were filled with flowers during the day and small scented lamps at night. The effect of color and light through the shimmering curtain of water was stunning and one of Shah Jahan's particular delights. He built such niches in his gardens at a change in level in the watercourse where water chutes had customarily been used.

The garden was divided into four plots by broad walks; in the center was a large platform surrounding a foliated pool. This was a bathing pool for the women as the Anguri Bagh was the zenana garden. Three other walls of the garden enclosure were composed of two-story palaces with dozens of little rooms opening onto the garden, looking much like an elegant dormitory.

The most unusual and interesting detail of the garden, however, is the stone curbing in a repeated geometric pattern which divides each of the four plots. This is the only Mughal garden to contain such curbing; its survival is nothing short of amazing. The plots were enclosed by sandstone fences carved in a whimsical, rustic pattern. Replicas for two sections have been carved, which today stand isolated at the front of the garden.

It is useful to compare the Anguri Bagh with the zenana garden of the Rajput palace at Amber. At Amber, the design of the central pool is a hexagram and the geometric pattern of the masonry divisions of the plots are thus based on its triangular components. Hexagrams are found repeatedly in the iconography of the Hindus, and the garden at Amber is a Hindu adaptation of a Mughal design.

Jahangir's mother was the princess of Amber, and, on occasion, he visited her

Amber. Zenana garden.
Section of hexagonal
pool and plots.

138

Amber. View of terraced garden within lake from private quarters of palace.

Rajput family. It is said Jahangir envied the beauty of the hillside palace begun by his uncle in 1600. From the private apartments at the top of the palace, there is a striking view of a lake garden far below which is still decorated with stone curbing. In nineteenth-century photographs, a dense growth of shade trees eclipses the patterns of stone, but viewed today from the heights of the palace one feels it was probably originally planted with flowers and meant to provide a colorful view from above.

The garden consists of three terraces of unequal size and unusual proportions. The highest terrace is a charbagh divided by a wide waterchannel and has a central, foliated, octagonal pool similar to that of Babur's Lotus Garden. At the end of the garden twelve rehants raised water from the lake to the highest level; it fell across a broad band of decorative niches between each terrace.

Some of the buildings in the Galta Pass below the Amber palace have chhatris with the bent eaves so popular in Rajputana. Havell claims this derived from bamboo structures and was brought to the Mughal court by Bengali craftsmen who then moved on to Rajputana.[15] Shah Jahan used the design in the Naulakha, a garden pavilion within the Lahore Fort built in 1633 and in the Golden Pavilion of the Agra Fort. Most Mughal pavilions, however, have deep, straight eaves.

Formally spaced, growing, flowering plants appear carved in relief in white marble and inlaid with semi-precious stones in the buildings of Shah Jahan. Robert Skelton has written of the introduction of this motif by Jahangir in manuscripts, and he makes an interesting connection to European herbals.[16] Very naturalistic in execution, the botanical detail is misleading; blossoms, foliage, height, and growing habits are often mixed, and many plants were hybrids created by the artists. Floral decoration continued to dominate the art of the Mughals and covered their saddles, shields, weapons, dishes, textiles, carpets, manuscripts, paintings, slippers and robes.

Lahore. Bent-roofed pavilion within fort.

Not only had the garden structures and palaces of the emperors become more elaborate, everything about court life became increasingly lavish. When the emperors moved between their fortress cities, they became a hazard for the population not to mention the damage they did to the countryside, for the royal retinue had swelled to a cumbersome procession several miles long. While crossing the Punjab in 1633, Shah Jahan found it necessary to order that "his archers should take charge of one side of the road, and the matchlockmen should guard the other so the growing crops should not be trampled underfoot by the followers of the royal train." [17]

When Babur marched from Kabul to the vicinity of Lahore in five weeks, the entire invading army and camp was 12,000 people. About ninety years after Babur's death on a campaign to the Deccan, it took Jahangir four months to travel 325 miles with a retinue which included 1,000 elephants alone—each with four attendants. Sir Thomas Roe, the first ambassador sent by the British Crown to promote trade with India, accompanied the emperor. He reported the tent city which surrounded the royal enclosure on this journey was a "little less than twenty English miles in circuit" and had streets, bazaars, markets, and mosques. [18] This traveling city did not disturb the emperor who rode ahead of the enormous train in order that he might hunt. In his *Memoirs,* Jahangir lyrically described these hunts: "On the banks of tanks or streams or large rivers in pleasant places which were full of trees and poppy fields in flower, and no day passed that I did not hunt while halting or travelling. Riding on horseback or on an elephant I came along the whole way looking about and hunting, and none of the difficulties of travelling were experienced; one might say that there was a change from one garden to another." [19]

These oriental military campaigns had slowed to become a royal progress often with predictably minor military success. They did, however, have some great political advantages. When the sovereign traveled, for sport or pleasure, he was accompanied by troops, preceded by standards, and heralded by the beat of the royal kettledrums. A "royal hunt" in a rebellious state was known to prevent uprisings. The pageantry accompanying the royal approach alone could instill fear in dissident local rulers, and they often fled. Jahangir often found it useful so to display Imperial power.[20] In some frequently troubled areas, it was convenient for him to build gardens at a suitable campsite where he could grant an audience to local dignitaries and rebellious chieftains. Occasionally, a mere announcement of an emperor's visit was enough to stop any local trouble.

The ability of Jahangir's gardeners to provide continuous bloom impressed Edward Terry, chaplain to Sir Thomas Roe who accompanied the ambassador on his travels in India: "Curious gardens, planted with fruitful trees and delightful flowers, to which Nature daily lends such a supply as that they seeme never to fade. In these places they have pleasant fountaynes to bathe in and other delights by sundrie conveyances of water, whose silent murmure helps to lay their sense with the bonds of sleepe in the hot seasons of the day."[21]

The lovely city of Lahore, capital of the Punjab, was considered one of the most important cities of the empire; it commanded the route to the north—the historic avenue of invasion in India. The high road north from Agra had shifted through the ages, but essentially the Great Mughal route was the Royal Road of the Mauryan Empire, and is today known as the Grand Trunk Road. Like the Mauryan rulers centuries before them, the Mughals maintained the route, bordered it with shade trees, and provided caravanserais, wells, and milestones for the safety and convenience of travelers and couriers.

There was a large Mughal garrison in Lahore, and the emperor regarded its governorship as important and always appointed a strong and loyal man. Within a two-day march of Lahore, there were dozens of royal charbaghs and halting places. Not only had Akbar held his court there from 1584 to 1598, and Jahangir visited frequently and been buried there, but several Mughal princes—brothers of the emperors—had established their courts there. For other princes, it was a place of sanctuary when fleeing disfavor at court. The gardens built by Mughal princes and nobles in Lahore reflect their fondness for reserving a garden for a special fruit: the Anguri (grape) Bagh, Badami (almond) Bagh, Anar (pomegranate) Bagh, and Nakhlia (date) Bagh.[22]

In 1641, Shah Jahan began construction of Shalamar Bagh, a great royal serai barely a day's march from the fortress in the city. Shalamar Bagh is not only the best surviving Mughal Paradise Garden, but the most magnificent example of any Mughal garden because of water which flows through and enlivens it. Daily almost four hundred fountains jet prismatic plumes four meters into the air, pools overflow, and water bubbles down the chaddar. Here the original grandeur of the lost water gardens can be appreciated.

In this great palatial serai, many of Shah Jahan's architectural ideas took shape. His pavilions here and in the Red Fort were not only similar in design, but were decorated with the same inlay work of semi-precious stones he had used in the Taj Mahal. In the eighteenth century, the garden was the scene of a battle and the inlaid polished marble facing of the buildings was looted. In the

SHALAMAR BAGH, LAHORE

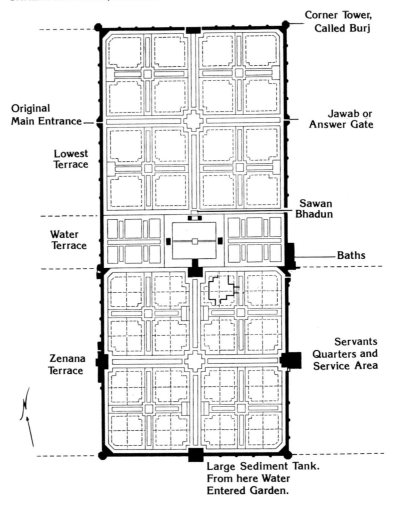

Corner Tower,
Called Burj

Original
Main Entrance

Jawab or
Answer Gate

Lowest
Terrace

Sawan
Bhadun

Water
Terrace

Baths

Servants
Quarters and
Service Area

Zenana
Terrace

Large Sediment Tank.
From here Water
Entered Garden.

N

Lahore. Reconstruction of Shalamar Bagh. (Archaeological Survey of India)

nineteenth century, it was a crumbling deserted ruin, but has now been rebuilt with great care and attention to detail.

Today, Shalamar covers almost forty acres and is divided into three terraces each ten feet above the next. The highest, the zenana terrace, and the lowest, the garden of public audience, are charbaghs of equal size, 730 feet square. The narrow central terrace, 200-feet-by-730-feet, is a water garden in three sections.

The two charbaghs are divided in the familiar four-fold pattern by canals twenty feet wide which are bordered on either side by twenty-foot-wide brick-paved walks. The quarters are subdivided by secondary waterchannels and narrower walks, forming sixteen plots in all.

As when they were built, the fountains throughout the garden have a single jet, and the glistening water shoots up almost four meters and drops back to

Shalamar. Marble waterchute between zenana terrace and water terrace.

form a rippling pattern on the water's surface. The main canal of the zenana terrace has a single line of fountains, the canal on the lowest terrace has a triple row. The original fountains, plundered from the channels, are thought to have been the marble lotus buds common to most Mughal gardens. These have been replaced by sandstone carved in that pattern.

At the end of the upper terrace, the water flows beneath a pavilion spanning the canal and overlooking the entire garden. Beneath it, water splashes down a wide, elegant marble chaddar and passes under the emperor's marble throne into the central reservoir of the middle terrace. Originally, 150 fountains set in the tank and along its foliated edge misted the water terrace. A small baradari on each side of the reservoir and plots shaped in the chain-pattern of Lahore, complete the central section of the water terrace. The waterchannels, pools, and walks of the flanking sections are being restored.

The chief beauty of the garden is the "sawan bhadun" through which the water flows from the water terrace to the lower charbagh. It is like a sunken room with three walls of water cascading in front of icy-white marble niches. The floor of the sawan bhadun has five fountains spraying silvery water. With bright flowers or twinkling lamps in the niches behind the curtains of water, it must have been breathtakingly beautiful. The fourth side of the sawan bhadun is an open narrow marble walkway, its roof supported by cusped marble arches. The water flows under this walk into the main canal of the lowest terrace. The sawan bhadun is named for the rainy season which brings such joy and creates such excitement on the dry sub-continent.

Because of its spaciousness, the garden—opulent and sensuous—must have had a languid air in spite of the birds, the music, and the vividly dressed courtiers.

143

Its spell was still irresistible in the spring of 1885 when the British viceroy and his lady, the Marchioness of Dufferin and Ava, attended an evening party at Shalamar: "Straight away from us went a pathway of water, down the centre of which played a succession of little fountains, giving a sort of misty mysteriousness to the scene. On either side of this fairy-like canal were broad bands of fire, and walks, and great rows of large trees with quantities of Chineses lanterns and various illuminating devices intermixed. These lines of fire and water crossed the gardens in every direction, and at the end of the first terrace we found ourselves in a sort of open colonnade ... on the other side of which we looked down upon another great illuminated water garden. It was too lovely . . . ."[23]

Two years later, the Vicereine, an admirable woman and usually a sensitive and intrepid traveler, must have been somewhat homesick, for following an afternoon visit to Shalamar she declared she would never have an Indian garden. "You can't think how damp and nasty they are. The beds are sunk instead of being raised and there are ditches cut round each one, and the walks are kept wet and muddy, and everything looks soaked and ugly. I can't imagine having any pleasure in such bogs as they become."[24] The Vicereine preferred a lawn, and the English, who succeeded the Mughals as foreign rulers in India, built great lawns in defiance of the climate. This English tradition, so picturesque in

Shalamar. Sahwan Bhavan.

144

Shalamar. View of lowest terrace through original main entrance of garden.

the misty isle, has a certain absurdity under the blazing sun of the Indian plains.

Throughout Shah Jahan's reign, most large Mughal building projects in Lahore were brick; the tile ornamentation was in the Persian manner. Good building stone could not be found in the area, so brick had replaced wood as the common building material. The high brick walls of the royal serai have polygonal towers, called *burj,* at the corners; the stuccoed interior walls are decorated with rows of huge shallow niches introduced by Akbar in his monumental gates.

The main entrance to Shalamar was through the central gate in the west wall of the lowest, or public, terrace. Some of the handsome gate's brilliantly colored dark-blue, yellow and white tile decoration remains. Opposite it, on the east wall, is the jawab, or answer gate, a false gateway traditionally built by the Mughals for symmetrical balance. Also built into the east wall between the zenana and water terrace is a humman. A large walled area east of the zenana terrace contained the kitchens, grooms and servants' quarters. Pavilions for the emperor, the queen, and other members of the royal family were on the zenana terrace.

Originally the garden had massed plantings of fruit trees favored by the Mughals. Today, the zenana terrace is planted with grass under large handsome shade trees and contains pots of gay flowers along the walks. The plantings are sparse on the other terraces where much restoration is underway. The cost of marble is so great that sandstone, carved in the style of the original marble, is being used.

From the Ravi River, a canal one hundred miles long brought water to a large complex of gardens which included Shalamar. Although the course of the Ravi was much closer to Lahore, this canal was necessary to maintain water pressure for the gravity-fed system. From the canal, water flowed through two gardens

145

before entering the huge sediment tank on the south side of the zenana terrace of Shalamar. Clay pipes carried the water to an aqueduct along the top of the garden's south wall and through the central zenana pavilion into the main waterchannel. From Shalamar, the water continued on to two other gardens.

The canal from the Ravi River was the inspiration of Shah Jahan's talented and imaginative engineer, Ali Mardan Khan, who also laid out Shalamar. A Persian who had governed Kandahar for the Persian Shah before joining Shah Jahan, he improved and built gardens in Kashmir, and, in the 1640s, he repaired and extended a late fourteenth-century canal to supply the water for Shahjahan-abad. In proposing the Ravi Canal he argued that it would "benefit the cultivation of the country through which it should pass." This is a rare instance of Mughal building benefiting the people. In fact, as the Mughal court grew larger and more opulent, the life of the farmer who supported the economy grew worse. The demands of the selfish ruling class outreached the resources of the country. In the reign of Shah Jahan when the empire appeared richest and most magnificent, it was, in fact, beginning to rot at its very core. Though not immediately apparent, the period of decline had begun.

Shah Jahan's son, the usurper Aurangzeb, was puritanical and hard working, but a zealot whose own policies defeated him. His austerity drove the gifted musicians and painters from court and lost him the loyalty of the Hindu leaders. Subsequent wars of succession depleted not just the Imperial family but the ranks of the nobility as well. The success of the empire depended totally upon the character and power of the emperor; hence its decline accelerated under the inferior men who ruled in later years. Though the dynasty lasted another century, the creative era—made possible by the adventurous spirit and vitality of Babur and the administrative genius of Akbar—had ended. The surviving painting and architecture of this short period—only 131 years—is a spectacular legacy.

Aurangzeb was crowned in Shalamar Bagh outside of Delhi on the old route to Lahore, one of the largest pleasure gardens built during the reign of Shah Jahan. Today acres of fruit trees cover the old plots in a maze-like arrangement, and a trace of the watercourse can be seen on but one ruined terrace. Bats cling to the broken exposed brick cupola of the one remaining chhatri, and the shed skins of serpents mingle with the broken trim of the foliated pool.

Visiting a restored Mughal garden can be a disorienting experience, for they bear no relation to the life or the land outside their crenellated walls. Of course, they never did. They are reminders of a foreign presence, like a crusader castle in the Levant or the Roman ruins in northern Britain.

Nomadic life does not produce an architecture, and the Persian architecture adopted by the Mughal's ancestors was, as we have seen, enriched by Indian themes and transformed by Indian craftsmen into a distinctive and exceptionally graceful style.

It is their pleasure gardens—great royal encampments—and the Paradise Gardens surrounding their tombs which were the most Mughal and the least Indian of anything they built. In the design of their gardens, the Mughals balanced everything perfectly: space and texture, light and shade, color and scent. In the realm of waterworks, their imaginations knew no bounds; every detail was considered, even surface patterns. In Kashmir, they covered the bottom of a

Plan of the Garden of Paradise
from the early eighteenth
century-Indian illustrated
manuscript, "Illustrated Guide
to Mecca and the Hereafter."
(Courtesy of the Curators of
the Bodleian Library, Oxford)

wide canal with rocks creating the illusion of a rushing brook, and carefully placed stones in a narrow channel so that the water would weave an intricate pattern. The returning jets of water from fountains created a delicate floral pattern on some pools.

Above all, it was the playful use of water in their gardens that so enchanted and pleased the Mughals. For these gardens were not just symbols of power where they lusted after pleasure. Rather, the deeper symbolism and the poetic nature of the appeal of these Paradise Gardens is reaffirmed in an inscription in the Red Fort describing the water garden of the palace: "The Hayat Bakhsh (life bestowing) garden, which is to these buildings as the soul is to the body, and the lamp to an assembly; and of the pure canal, the limpid water of which is to the person possessing sight, as a mirror showing the world; and of the water cascades, each of which you may see is the whitener of the dawn . . . . and of the fountains, each of which is a hand of light inclined to shake hands with the inhabitants of heavens, or a string of bright pearls made to descend to reward the inhabitants of earth; and of the tank, full to the brim of water of life and in its purity the envy of light and the spring of the sun."

147

Epilogue

As the Mughal Empire weakened, its architecture declined. Many small states in northern India—Hindu and Muslim—grew stronger and their rulers built grand palaces and gardens, which were usually adaptations of the Mughal style. These palace gardens lacked strong axial symmetry, and the use of water in them diminished; they were no longer built as charbaghs.

After charbaghs ceased to be built, however, they were represented in paintings. Aurangzeb's ban against painting following his ascension in 1657 resulted in the dispersal of the Mughal court painters to provincial courts and the establishment of many fine schools of painting in India. Gardens were a favorite mise-en-scene for the artists. While the paintings are frequently characterized by their fine portraits and contain realistic detail, the settings are often idealized. A lovely garden with fountains and flowers in geometric plots was a favorite background for the Indian artist as was the idealized garden of eternal spring for the Persian painter.

During the great Mughal period, which ended with the death of Shah Jahan, many other noteworthy gardens were built. In 1559, the Rana of Mewar was driven from his citadel at Chitor and established his capital at Udaipur. The independent Mewaris took advantage of the beautiful natural surroundings in the Aravali Hills and built some of the most charming palaces and gardens in India.

In 1725, the Jat ruler of Bharatpur state began construction of a great palace and "Mughal" garden at Dig. Forty years later when the Jats raided the Fort at Agra, marble fountains and other garden fixtures were part of the booty taken for the Dig garden. The gardens at Dig are the loveliest of the Mughal-style gardens built after Pinjaur. Situated between two huge tanks, the spacious palaces surround a charbagh lined with tall shady trees encircled by wide grass platforms. One delightful pavilion is curtained with water from three rows of jets and fountains and by water falling from the eaves. This creates the impression of a rainstorm—an event which gladdens all Indian hearts. To this is added the thrill of thunder: water is forced up a hollow pillar, causing large stone balls to roll around in the ceiling. This extensive water garden is supplied by four Persian wheels which raise the water to a massive tank at the level of the palace roof. Wooden plugs in the tank walls control the flow of water into the gravity-fed system. Boys swim in the tank for the purpose of pulling the plugs which open the pipelines to the fountains and water devices.

With the restoration of the Mughal monuments has come a renewed interest in the gardens. The Rashtrapati Bhavan, now the official residence of the president of India, was designed by Sir Edwin Lutyens as the Vice-Regal Palace and was completed in 1929. Much of the palace complex of 300 acres is composed of formal gardens. In these attractive and well-kept gardens, the waterchannels are derived from Mughal design. There are also a number of external influences, however: a moon gate, a circular sunken garden, and stretches of lawn rather than symmetrical groupings of fruit trees.

Similar external influences can be seen in modern adaptations of the Paradise Gardens in Iran. There is currently a particular interest in the old gardens, and vanishing gardens are being preserved and restored. Recently there has been a great deal of quality restoration; painstaking attention is being given to original design, materials, color, and finish.

The design of the Persian garden has persisted and become diffused throughout the world. In America, we can see the Persian ancestry in some of the old Spanish mission gardens; the first date palm in California was said to have been planted in 1770 by Franciscans newly arrived from Spain. The landscape of the American Southwest resembles that of the high plateau of Iran; the mission gardens must have had the same appeal for wayfarers in the American desert as the old Paradise Gardens had for the weary travelers in Persia.

"Scenes of Paradise," Rajasthan, 1825–1850. Unusual painting in which a central white area represents celestial space surrounded by a series of gardens. (Collection of Paul Walter)

149

Alwar. The City Palace is a group of later buildings showing much Mughal influence; however, they overlook a large tank rather than a garden. Unlike the Hindus who built impressive stairways at their tanks, the Mughals never made stairways a prominent feature of their architecture. The exception is at Akbar's victory gate at Fathepur Sikri.

The earliest book on Indian plants, the *Hortus Indicus Malabaricus*, was published in Amsterdam in 1668, twenty years after the death of Shah Jahan. It was compiled from material supplied by H. A. van Rheede tot Draakestein, the Dutch governor of Malabar and illustrated by plates drawn by a Neapolitan priest. In the spirit of Alexander's Eastern expedition in the fourth century B.C., European botanical explorers began identifying and collecting Eastern plants in the seventeenth century. Our information about plants in the early gardens is at present incomplete. For more specific information, we must look forward to the findings of paleobotanists as exploration of sites in India and Iran continues.

Appendix

Gardening Notes

Abul Fazl, Akbar's friend and the historian of his reign, left a four-volume work describing the court, the administration of the empire, and the achievements and virtues of the emperor. He has told us everything there is to know about elephant harnesses, but nothing about gardening. He does mention the imperial kitchen garden for fresh greens, and he describes some Indian flowers; however, the only details of cultivation he recorded were for sugar cane and the betel nut.

An insect called the "white ant" (though not truly an ant) is a scourge in India and has seriously damaged or completely destroyed most of the records from early Mughal times. Therefore, we have to depend on oral tradition for much of our information on gardening practices.

In India today, the Malis, or gardeners, say they garden the same way their ancestors did for the Mughals. That may well be so, for some things change little; their ancestors were gardeners, and their methods certainly have not been influenced by the technological revolution. Except for the lawn mower, there are few machines in use. It is a curious sight to see an Indian lawn being mowed; the heavy machines are pushed and pulled by a team of three, sometimes four, men, or a man and a bullock.

Gardens are still watered by flooding as they were under Akbar and when Lady Dufferin visited Shalamar. This softens the soil sufficiently to enable earthworms to work their way to the surface, and thus aerate the soil. The pools of water can evaporate before one's eyes, and the ground bakes very hard. (There is no common practice of mulching.) The malis must break up the soil; for this they employ their all-purpose tool, the *khurpi,* a small hand hoe. Rakes are not used. Malis sweep the gardens and lawns with handsome brooms made up of bunches of twigs. Insects are a problem, and Malis prefer portable gardens in big red clay pots. It is customary before planting shrubs to burn leaves in the hole to discourage grubs.

Unlike the Mughal period, everything is now pruned very severely. In northern India, the roses bloom three times a year. However, they are cut back constantly, so the rose gardens alternate between riotous color and stiff leafless shrubs.

Abul Fazl (ca. 1565) composed a list of some "fine smelling flowers," and in his book, *Beautiful Gardens*, Dr. M. S. Randhawa has recently composed a list of flowers, shrubs and trees suited to a moonlight garden. I find the most beautiful flowers in India to be the brilliant blossoms on the native Indian flowering trees.

A List of Fine Smelling Flowers

—from *Ain I Akbari*
by Abul Fazl (Allama),
translated by H. Blochmann.

1. The **Sewti.** Whitish; blooms the whole year, especially toward the end of the rains.
2. The **Bholsari.** Whitish; in the rains.
3. The **Chambeli.** White, yellow, and blue. In the rains, and partly during winter.
4. **Raibel.** White and pale yellow. In the end of the hot season, and the beginning of the rains.
5. The **Mongra.** Yellow. In summer.
6. The **Champah.** Yellow. All the year; especially when the sun stands in Pisces and Aries.
7. **Ketki.** Upper leaves green, inner ones yellowish-white. Blooms during hot season.
8. **Kuzah.** White. During the hot season.
9. The **Padal.** Brownish lilac. In spring.
10. The **Juhi.** White and yellow, like jasmin. During the rains.
11. The **Niwari.** Whitish. In spring.
12. The **Nargis.** White. In spring.
13. The **Kewarah.** From Leo to Libra.
14. The **Chaltah.**
15. The **Gulal.** In spring.
16. The **Tasbih i Gulal.** White. In winter.
17. The **Singarhar.** It has small white petals. In the hot season.
18. The **Violet.** Violet. In the hot season.
19. The **Karnah.** White. In spring.
20. The **Kapur bel.**
21. The **Gul i Za'faran.** Lilac. In autumn.

Malis, *ca.* 1800 or earlier. Malis today: plant, weed, and trim in this same position.
(Private collection)

The Vegetation of the Earthly Garden

"The Vegetation of the Earthly Garden," a list of vegetation which appears in poetic descriptions of gardens and garden imagery, was compiled and appended by William L. Hanaway, Jr. to his paper in the Fourth Dumbarton Oaks Colloquium, the *Islamic Garden,* in 1976. Mr. Hanaway points out that his list is not exhaustive, and, as an example of the difficulty of precisely identifying flowers, mentions that flowers of different descriptions are sometimes called by the same Persian name, while some single flowers have multiple names.

The following is a selection from Mr. Hanaway's list:

Persian name	English	Figurative meaning
Anar	Pomegranate	the breasts
'Ar'ar	Juniper	beloved's figure
Arghavan	Judas tree	the face
Badam	Almond	the eye
Bih, bihi	Quince	the chin
Bih danih	Quince seed	mole or beauty spot
Bihisht	(Garden of) Paradise	the face
Bustan	garden	the face
Chenar	Plane-tree	its leaf is likened to the human hand
Ghunchih	bud	the breast, lips
Gul	Rose; any flower	breast or bosom; cheek; face
Gulshan	garden	the face
Gulzar	garden	the face
Jannat	Garden of Paradise	the face
Lalih	Tulip	the face, cheek
Limu	Lemon	the breasts, chin
Marzanjush	Forget-me-not	hair, down
Mihrgiah	Mandrake	down
Murd	Myrtle	hair
Nai	reed, Bamboo	beloved's figure
Naishakar	Sugarcane	beloved's figure
Nakhl	Date palm	beloved's figure
Nargis	Narcissus	the eye
Narvan	Elm	beloved's figure
Nasrin	White Rose	face, chin, bosom, teeth
Nastaran	Eglantine	the face
Sarv	Cypress	the beloved; the beloved's figure
Sib	Apple	the chin
Shikufih	blossom	the teeth
Sunbul	Hyacinth	hair, cheek, down
Tuba	a tree of Paradise	beloved's figure
Turanj	Citron	the breasts, chin
Yasmin	Jasmine	face, hair, bosom

153

Notes

Introduction

1. Xenophon, *The Oeconomicus*, trans. by Carnes Lord, from *Xenophon's Socratic Discourse, An Interpretation of the Oeconomicus*, Leo Strauss (Ithaca and London: 1970), pp. 19–22.

2. See Paradise, Oxford English Dictionary (Oxford: 1933), Vol. VII.

3. We cannot be completely certain of the plant material used.

4. It should be kept in mind that modern concepts and meanings for terms such as fertility, or even garden, may differ greatly from those of ancient man.

5. Samuel Noah Kramer, *From the Tablets of Sumer* (Indian Hills, Colo.: 1956), pp. 172–173.

6. R. deRohan Barondes, *Garden of the Gods, Mesopotamia 5,000 B.C.* (Boston), pp. 195–196.

7. The word "Paradise" was unknown to Homer who wrote more than 1,000 years before Xenophon.

8. See Mircea Eliade, *Myths, Dreams and Mysteries; the Encounter Between Contemporary Faiths and Archaic Realities* (New York: 1961), chap. on "Nostalgia for Paradise in the Primitive Traditions," pp. 59–72.

9. Corinthians II (12:2—4).

10. There are about 120 references to gardens in the Koran.

11. S. N. Kramer, op. cit, p. 68. See also S. N. Kramer, *Gilgamesh and the Huluppu Tree.*

12. Phyllis Ackerman, *Survey of Persian Art*, Vol. I, p. 845. See also P. Ackerman, "The Moon and Fertility in Iran," *Bulletin of the American Institute for Persian Art and Archaeology* (1937), Vol. V, pp. 184–189.

13. See Paul Underwood, "The Fountain of Life in Manuscripts of the Gospels," *Dumbarton Oaks Papers* (Washington: 1950), Vol. V, pp. 41–48.

14. Edward Hyams, *Soil and Civilization* (New York: 1976), p. 35.

15. Thousands of clay tablets 4,500 years old have been excavated from the recently discovered ruins of Ebla; among those deciphered are tablets listing plants. See Bermant and Weitzman, *Ebla: A Revelation in Archaeology* (London: 1979).

16. Roman Ghirshman, *Iran: from the Earliest Times to the Islamic Conquest* (Penguin: 1954), pp. 34, 40.

17. Farming settlements which continued throughout several millennia have been found on the Iranian plateau in the Holy Land, in Anatolia and the Zagros Mountains; after the fifth millennium, however, civilization in the Near East was dominated by lower Mesopotamia.

18. Introduction to *Survey of Persian Art* (London: 1938), Vol. I.

19. The Paradise Garden has had great influence on Western literature and has been an inspiration to Western poets from the ancient Greeks to the Renaissance. See also A. Bartlett Giamatti, *The Earthly Paradise and the Renaissance Epic*, and Charles L. Sanford, *The Quest for Paradise* in which he discusses the depth of the search for Paradise in American civilization. As evidence of the universal nature of the concept of Paradise as a garden, it is interesting to note that in Japanese the word "Paradise" is composed of two characters: one meaning enjoying, the other meaning garden. In the pictograph of the word garden, a wall encloses three figures.

Chapter One

1. David Stronach, *Pasargadae*, A report on the excavations conducted by the British Institute of Persian Studies from 1961–1963 (Oxford: 1978), pp. 108–112.

2. Victoria Sackville-West, "Persian Gardens" in A. J. Arberry, ed., *Legacy of Persia* (Oxford: 1953), p. 287.

3. Arrian, *Anabasis of Alexander*, trans. by E. Iliff Robson, Loeb Classical Library (London and New York: 1953), Vol. VI, chap. 28., p. 195.

4. Ibid., p. 197.

5. Strabo, *The Geography*, Loeb Classical Library (London and New York: 1930), Vol. XV, pp. 7–8, 167.

6. Plutarch, *Parallel Lives* (New York: 1931), p. 571.

7. Xenophon, *Cyropaedia*, trans. by Walter Miller (London and New York: 1925), p. 39.

8. Egyptian tomb paintings of the Eighteenth Dynasty are rich in details of daily life, many picturing gardens. Scholars have detected Mesopotamian influence in secular life in Egypt by this era, but no comparable record of gardens exists in Western Asia, therefore a useful comparison cannot be made.

9. Arthur Upham Pope, *Survey of Persian Art* (Oxford: 1938), Vol. I, p. 114.

10. Pyllis Ackerman, *Survey of Persian Art* (Oxford: 1938), Vol. I, p. 845.

11. Herzfeld and Keith in *Iran as a Prehistoric Center* make a fascinating claim regarding the battle of Salamis: "The old Iranian civilization died at Salamis, the most momentous event in the history of mankind, which decided between Asia and Europe. Every stone at Persepolis tells the story. When the Greeks under Alexander the Great conquered Iran, all its vitality had vanished. The conquest was a consequence, not the cause, of the irreparable decay. Iran completely surrendered to Europeanization. But it never accepted the spirit of Europe, and so the process of elimination soon begins; a reaction sets in and Iran turns back again to a revival of its own true nature."

12. J. S. McCrindle, Pliny in *Alexander's Invasion of India* (Calcutta: 1882).

13. Roman Ghirshman, *Iran* (Penguin: 1954), p. 182.

14. Though the Persians knew how to prune trees very early, they did so judiciously and allowed the trees to grow naturally, unlike the ancient Egyptians who pruned them severely.

15. Plutarch, *Vitae Parallelae*, Loeb Classical Library (London and New York: 1914), Vol. XI, p. 131.

16. Polybius, Loeb Classical Library, Vol. X, p. 25.

17. Mentioned frequently by Sir Aurel Stein, *Archaeological Reconnaissances in N. W. India and S. E. Iran* (London: 1937).

18. Sir John Malcolm, *Sketches of Persia*, 2 Vols. (London: 1828), Vol. I, p. 57.

Chapter Two

1. Roman Ghirshman, *Iran* (Penguin: 1954), p. 239.

2. Plutarch, *Vitae Parallelae, Life of Lucullus*, Loeb Classical Library (London and New York: 1914), Vol. II, p. 599.

3. G. Le Strange, *Lands of the Eastern Caliphate* (Cambridge: 1905). A translation and compilation of the Arab geographers and historians.

4. Ibid., p. 255, also p. 294.

5. Richard N. Frye, *The Heritage of Persia* (Cleveland and New York: 1963), p. 214.

6. Lars Ivar Ringbom, *Paradisus Terrestris* (Helsinki: 1958). An English summary will be found on pp. 435–446, and the more than two hundred illustrations have English captions.

7. Oscar Reuther, *Survey of Persian Art* (Oxford: 1938), Vol. I, p. 493.

8. According to Charles Grant Ellis, the noted authority on carpets, the oldest surviving garden carpet is that known as the Jaipur carpet in the State Museum, Jaipur, India, believed to be of the late seventeenth century. Mr. Ellis has a book forthcoming on garden carpets, written in collaboration with Donald N. Wilber.

9. Tabiri, Tarikh ur Rusul Wal Muluk, *History of the Prophets and Kings*, usually referred to as *The Annals*. Tabiri claims the scraps of the "Spring of Khusrau" were sold to a jeweler in Baghdad for the equivalent of $3,000. each, making the total original value of the carpet over $200,000,000.

10. Edward Gibbon, *Decline and Fall of the Roman Empire* (London: 1909–1913), Vol. 8, pp. 229–230.

11. C. James Rich, *Narrative of a Residence in Koordistan* (edited by his widow), Vol. II, pp. 263–267.

Chapter Three

1. H. A. R. Gibb, *Mohammedanism*, second edition with revisions (London and New York: 1975), p. 3.

2. Edward H. Schafer, *Golden Peaches of Samarkand* (1963), p. 10.

3. There are well over one hundred references to gardens in the Koran. See also A. J. Arberry, *The Koran Reinterpreted*, and an older trans. by George Sale.

4. See Oleg Grabar, "The Umayyad Dome of the Rock in Jerusalem," *Ars Orientalis* (1959), Vol. 3, pp. 33–62.

5. Richard Ettinghausen, *Arab Painting* (New York: 1977), p. 42.

6. See K. A. C. Creswell, *Early Muslim Architecture*, 2 Vols (Oxford: 1952–1959).

7. John D. Hoag, *Western Islamic Architecture* (New York: 1963), p. 19.

8. Marie L. Gotheim, *History of Garden Art*, Vol. I, p. 150.

9. The painting decoration of the chapel of the royal palace, built in 1140, shows much Persian influence. See Ugo Monneret de Villard, *Cappella Palatina in Palermo* (Rome: 1950). Note particularly the ceiling panel of two musicians beside a wall fountain.

10. W. Knight, *Pictures from Sicily* (London: 1835), p. 160.

11. For a detailed description of Alhambra, see Oleg Grabar, *The Alhambra* (Cambridge: 1978), pp. 117–132.

12. A good example is the small stone lion in the Tehran Museum of Antiquities.

13. Anne Marie Schimmel, *The Celestial Garden in Islam*, Dumbarton Oaks Colloquium, Vol. IV, p. 26.

14. William L. Hanaway, Jr., *Paradise on Earth: The Terrestrial Garden in Persian Literature,* Dumbarton Oaks Colloquium, Vol. IV. In his chapter, Mr. Hanaway makes an interesting comparison between the plan of the *Gulistan* and a garden. See pp. 60–61. This was evidently inspired by Donald Wilber in "Iran, Bibliographical Spectrum," *Review of National Literature.*

Chapter Four

1. Dr. Maurizio Tosi, quoted by Sylvia A. Matheson in her excellent book, *Persia: An Archaeological Guide* (London: 1976), p. 278.

2. Bernard Lewis, *The Assassins* (London: 1967), in his interesting study on the Assassins cites Marco Polo, see p. 11.

3. E. J. W. Gibb, *History of Ottoman Poetry,* 6 Vols. (London: Luzac & Co., 1900), Vol. 1, pp. 6, 7.

4. Ralph Pinder-Wilson, *The Persian Garden: Bagh and Chahar Bagh* (Dumbarton Oaks Colloquium), Vol. IV, pp. 76–77.

5. Malleson, *Herat, The Granary and Garden of Central Asia,* trans. by Abdul Ruzzak (London: 1836).

6. Nizami Arudi Samarquandi, "Four Discourses," trans. by E. G. Browne in James Kritzeck, ed., *Anthology of Islamic Literature* (Penguin Books: 1964), p. 202.

7. Qasim ibn Yusuf Abu Nasri Haravi, *Irshad Az Zara-ah* (Herat: 1515), chap. 8, is the suggested lay-out of a chaharbagh. Ralph Pinder-Wilson has translated and summarized the chapter and included a schematic drawing in his chapter on the Persian garden, Ibid. 4.

8. Robert Byron, *Road to Oxiana* (London: 1950), p. 101.

9. Marco Polo, *The Travels,* trans. by Ronald Latham (Penguin Books: 1976), p. 57.

Chapter Five

1. Mirza Haidar, Tarkh-i Rashidi, *A History of the Moghuls,* trans. by E. Denison Ross (Patna: 1973), p. 232. Mirza Haidar was Babur's young cousin and was raised by Babur for a few years. His account of the Mughal history is fascinating.

2. Safavid fighting men wore a distinctive twelve-gored conical red hat representing the twelve immans of Islam. This identified them as Shiites and is the source of the name *Kazilbash*, or redheads by which they were known.

3. It has been suggested by some historians, including Sir Percy M. Sykes, that Jenkinson's account of Persia was the source of Milton's references to the Sophi in *Paradise Lost.*

4. Roger Stevens, *The Land of the Great Sophy* (London: 1971), p. 185.

5. Sir Robert Ker Porter, *Travels,* 2 Vols. (London: 1821), Vol. I, p. 419. The author was the court artist in Russia, and the book is beautifully illustrated with drawings.

6. Sir John Chardin, *Travels in Persia,* trans. by E. Lloyd (London: 1927), based on a 1720 edition. Chardin was a native of France, but following his travels in the East, he settled in England and was knighted by Charles II; he then became jeweler to the court.

7. The Tehran Archaeological Museum has an excellent collection of artifacts. See, particularly, the small stone Achaemenid lion.

8. Chardin, usually a reliable observer, estimated that Isfahan had 273 baths, 162 mosques, 48 madrassas or Muslim theological colleges, 12 cemeteries and a staggering 1,802 caravanserais.

9. One of the buildings built into the wall of the Bagh-i Fin is now a museum housing some interesting findings from the excavations at Siyalk.

10. Sir Thomas Herbert, *A Relation of Some Years Travaile* (London: 1652). A facsimile reprint (Da Capo Press; Austria and New York: 1971), p. 92.

11. Lord Curzon, *Persia and the Persian Question*, 2 Vols. (London: 1892), Vol. I, p. 275.

12. Experienced lead camels were highly prized on the silk route to China for this ability as mentioned by Edward H. Schafer.

13. Herbert, op. cit., p. 91.

14. Ibid. Sir Thomas must have been carried away by his arrival at the garden in the midst of the salt desert. There is no trace of a "grotto," nor any other mention of evidence to support his romantic account of echoes, grottoes and labyrinths.

15. Shah Abbas also founded an Armenian Christian community at Julfa, across the river from Isfahan. Today, one of the large old Julfa houses is an institute teaching restoration techniques. Part of the curriculum is devoted to gardens.

16. Curzon, op. cit., Vol. II, p. 503.

Chapter Six

1. Mircea Eliade, *Shamanism, Archaic Techniques of Ecstasy*, trans. by Willard R. Trask (Pantheon Books: 1964). It is in this work that symbols, myths and rites of Shamanism are discussed in detail.

2. Apparently one of the Great Khan's strictures was against walls.

3. Although both the Turks and Mongols originated in the East, they spoke different languages. The Turks had migrated westward and had settled in Central Asia earlier than the more nomadic Mongols.

4. Ahmed Ibn Arabshah, *Timur, the Great Amir*, trans. by J. H. Sanders (London: 1936), p. 310.

5. Ibid., p. 6

6. Ibid., p.6.

7. Ibid., in some instances, more characteristically direct Turkish names such as "Meadow of the Plough" were used.

8. Ruy Gonzalez de Clavijo, *Embassy to Tamerlane*, trans. by Guy Le Strange (London: 1928), p. 220.

9. Ibid., p. 230.

10. Dr. Galina A. Pugachenkova, "The Art of Central Asian Gardens and Parks in the Time of Tamerlane and The Timurids," Works of the Central Asian State University, Ministry of Higher Education (Tashkent; USSR: 1951), pp. 143–168. (In Russian.)

11. Clavijo, op. cit., p. 288.

12. Ibid., p. 286.

13. Guy Le Strange, *Lands of the Eastern Caliphates* (Cambridge: 1905), p. 13.

14. C. C. Walker, *The History of Jenghiz Khan* (London: 1939), p. 93.

Chapter Seven

1. Annette Susannah Beveridge, *The Babur-Nama* (London: 1969), p. 74.

2. The exact meaning of the word *Narwan* has eluded translators.

3. Beveridge, op. cit., p. 81.

4. Ibid., p. 203.

5. Ibid., pp. 216–217.

6. Babur observed the Muslim practice of not burying the dead in land acquired by violence or wrong.

7. The difficulty in fixing exact names can be seen by reading Mrs. Beveridge's Appendix E on the subject (p. xvii). In it, she holds that Babur's *Adinapur* is a corruption of an earlier name *Udyanapur* meaning garden-town. The major deforestation of Afghanistan took place during the Mongol invasions beginning in 1218.

8. Beveridge, op. cit., pp. 208–209.

9. Ibid., p. 414.

10. Arrian, the *Anabasis of Alexander*, trans. by E. Iliff Robson, Book V (London and New York: 1933), p. 9.

11. Tuzuk-i-Jahangiri, or *Memoirs of Jahangir*, trans. by Alexander Rogers, Henry Beveridge, ed., 2 Vols. (Delhi: 1958), Vol. I, p. 125.

12. Beveridge, op. cit., p. 647.

13. In keeping with Babur's wishes, no building was erected over his grave until recent years when a stark, modern pavilion was built. Undoubtedly built for protection, it is an unfortunate addition, out of keeping with the site and his wishes.

14. Beveridge, op. cit., p. 525.

Chapter Eight

1. Paper prepared by Professor Diana L. Eck, "Ganga: The Goddess in Hindu Sacred Geography," Harvard University.

2. In Hindu belief, the primal condition was water; all life existed in water; there was no light. There are several versions of the creation myth, and the descent of the heavenly waters of life. In one variation, the celestial waters split into four parts at *Mt. Meru*, and ran out upon lotus-petal continents; one river became the Ganga (the Ganges).

3. The goddesses with water jugs are very like the Persian goddess, Anahita.

4. M. S. Randhawa, *Beautiful Gardens*, Indian Council of Agricultural Research (New Delhi: 1971), p. 69.

5. Megasthenes, "Indica," trans. by J. W. McCrindle, *Ancient India as Described by Megasthenes and Arrian* (Calcutta: 1877).

6. The satrap of the Indus valley paid the highest tribute to the Persian king.

7. It was pepper, more than any other spice, which first brought Western merchants to India. In one year, 1585, 1,750 tons were brought to Lisbon by Portuguese traders.

8. Arrian, *Indica*, trans. by E. Iliff Robson (London, New York), Book VIII, 10.2, p. 335.

9. For the description and examples of early Indian arches, see chapter on arches in Percy Brown, *Indian Architecture, Buddhist and Hindu* (Bombay: 1971).

10. The Persians required fast-setting gypsum mortar, because they had so little wood for centering. In addition to horsehair, the Indians added juggery, an unrefined brown sugar, which retarded the setting. Lime mortar was used as early as the Besnagar temple, second century B. C. (ASI Report: 1913–1914), p. 205.

11. Heinrich Zimmer, *Myths and Symbols in Indian Art and Civilization*, Joseph Cambell, ed., a section on the serpent motif, pp. 62–68. Identified as originally Mesopotamian, the device of intertwined serpents Dr. Zimmer believed to be non-Vedic and pre-Aryan: "The motif must have been diffused into India at an extremely remote era, before the arrival of the Aryans."

Chapter Nine

1. Annette S. Beveridge, *The Babur-Nama in English* (London: 1969), p. 465.

2. British engineers working on canal projects in the nineteenth century reported that some of the waters of the area near the Ghaggar were unhealthy and promoted disease.

3. Beveridge, op. cit., p. 484.

4. Ibid, p. 519. The term, "true rains" refers to the southwest monsoon.

5. In 1901, Lord Curzon appointed Sir John Marshall as Director General of the Archaeological Survey. In addition to surveying and listing the monuments of India, restoration and excavations were carried out—including the discovery of ancient cities in the Indus valley.

6. The custom at the court of Timur was to present gifts in sets of nine.

7. Beveridge, op. cit., p. 533.

8. Ibid., p. 532.

9. Ibid., p. 505.

10. Ibid., p. 532.

11. Henry Beveridge, ed., *The Tuzuk-i-Jahangiri, or Memoirs of Jahangir,* trans. by Alexander Rogers, 2 Vols. (Delhi: 1968), Vol. I, p. 4.

12. Ibid., II, p. 95.

13. Abul Fazl, Akbar's biographer, has an interesting note on Babur's garden: "On the opposite side of the river is the Char Bagh, a memorial of Babar. It was the birthplace of the writer of this work, and the last resting-place of his grandfather and his elder brother ... many other saintly personages also repose there." *Ain I Akbari,* trans. by Col. H. S. Jarrett (Calcutta: 1891), Vol. II, p. 180.

14. Beveridge, op. cit., p. 532.

15. Ibid., p. 610.

16. The measurement "10" in these accounts is based on a gaz. Ten-by-ten would be approximately twenty-three feet.

17. Beveridge, op. cit., p. 606.

18. Ibid., p. 615.

19. Ibid., p. 634.

20. Ibid., p. 639.

21. Ibid., p. 642.

22. The aqueduct which brought water from the square well has disappeared; its remains may be buried in the fields.

23. Gulbadan, *Humayun-Nama,* trans. by Annette S. Beveridge (London: 1902), p. 26.

24. E. M. Forster, *Abinger Harvest* (New York: 1936), p. 304.

Chapter Ten

1. Jauhar, *Tadhkirat al-Waqiat,* trans. by Charles Stewart (London: 1832), p. 65.

2. Abul Fazl, *The Akbar Nama,* trans. by Henry Beveridge (Calcutta: 1907), Vol. I, p. 648.

3. The existing walls are probably by Humayun with additions by Sher Shah.

4. Even Babur believed in some magic, i.e., the old Central Asian belief that a jade stone brought rain. See pp. 67, 654 of the *Babur-Nama.*

Chapter Eleven

1. Abul Fazl, *Akbar-Nama,* p. 105. Humayun had carried the manuscript of the *Babur-Nama* with him during his years of exile, and it was among the manuscripts which formed the beginning of the famous Mughal library.

2. Abul Fazl, *Akbar-Nama*, trans. by Henry Beveridge (Calcutta: 1907), Vol. 2, p. 576.

3. James Tod, *Annals and Antiquities of Rajast'han*, 2 Vols. (New Delhi: 1971), Vol. I, p. 613.

Chapter Twelve

1. Henry Beveridge, ed., *The Tuzuk-i-Jahangiri*, or *Memoirs of Jahangir*, trans. by Alexander Rogers (Delhi: 1968), Vol. II, p. 143.

2. Ibid., pp. 150–151.

3. Ibid., p. 162.

4. Ibid, Vol. I, p. 93.

5. Ibid., pp. 177–178.

6. Ibid., p. 143.

7. Ibid., p. 145.

8. Milo Cleveland Beach, *The Grand Mogul* (Williamstown: 1978), p. 27.

9. William Howard Adams, *The French Garden* (New York: 1979), p. 84.

10. Mughal architecture made no lasting influence in Kashmir as the Kashmiris continued to build in the native style; but Mughal design dominates the decorative arts and textiles of Kashmir.

11. François Bernier, *Travels in the Mogul Empire*, trans. by Archibald Constable (Delhi: 1968), p. 399.

12. Ibid., p. 400.

13. Vicomte Robert d'Humieres, *Through Isle and Empire* (New York: 1905), pp. 214–215.

14. W. H. Nochols in the Archaeological Survey Report on Mughal Gardens at Srinigar, 1906, details their decrepit conditions at the time. He particularly mentions that the stone waterchannels remained.

15. H. Beveridge, ed., op. cit., I, p. 94.

16. Ibid., p. 228.

Chapter Thirteen

1. There are many examples; for one, Ulugh Beg in Samarkand was a victim of parricide, but his son himself was murdered not long after his crime.

2. Annette S. Beveridge, *The Babur-Nama in English* (London: 1969), p. 702.

3. For a new and interesting interpretation of the Taj Mahal, see "The Myth of the Taj Mahal, and a New Theory of Its Symbolic Meaning" by Wayne E. Begley, *The Art Bulletin* (March: 1979).

4. In some sections of India, coconuts, rather than a lotus bud, can be seen on temple spires.

5. This is the conclusion of Mr. M. H. Siddique, Director of the Archaeological Survey of India, Northern Circle, following his investigation of the site.

6. R. Nath, *The Immortal Taj Mahal* (Bombay: 1972), p. 86.

7. In December 1974, Mr. M. Singh, Director of Gardens, Archaeological Survey of India, generously showed the existing supply system and explained the waterworks of the Taj to the author.

8. R. Nath, op. cit., p. 60.

9. François Bernier, *Travels in the Mogul Empire*, trans. by A. Constable (Delhi: 1968), p. 243.

10. It is likely "grottoes" refers to a baoli.

11. Bernier, op. cit., p. 267.

12. Captain Robert Smith, *Pictorial Journal of Travels in Hindustan,* Vol. II, p. 407.

13. There is now an electric pump with a tin roof in the baoli. This makes it difficult to see, but it is worth the effort.

14. Dr. Saifur Rahman Dar, "Some Ancient Gardens of Lahore," a pamphlet of Popular Publishers (Lahore: 1977), p. 10.

15. E. B. Havell, *Indian Architecture* (Delhi: S. Cahng and Co., 1972), p. 128.

16. Robert Skelton, "A Decorative Motif in Mughal Art," *Aspects of Indian Art* (Leiden: 1972), pp. 148-152.

17. H. M. Elliott, *The History of India, As Told By Its Own Historians,* John Dowson, ed., from the *Padshah-Nama* of Muhammad Amin Kazwini (London: 1877), Vol. VII, p. 43.

18. Sir William Foster, ed., *The Embassy of Sir Thomas Roe to India* (London: 1926), p. 324.

19. Henry Beveridge, ed., *The Tuzuk-i-Jahangiri, or Memoirs of Jahangir,* trans. by Alexander Rogers, 2 Vols. (Delhi: 1968), Vol. I, p. 363.

20. An example would be Jahangir's trip to Kabul in 1607, planned because of his border clash with Shah Abbas of Persia.

21. W. Foster, ed., *Early Travels in India* (London: 1921), p. 303.

22. Dr. S. Rahman Dar, op. cit., p. 6.

23. Lady Harriot Dufferin, *Our Viceregal Life in India,* 2 Vols., (London: 1889), Vol. I, p. 121.

24. Ibid., Vol. II, p. 227. Lady Dufferin worked hard and effectively in India for better medical treatment for the poor.

SELECTED BIBLIOGRAPHY

The literature devoted to Persian and Mughal gardens is not extensive:

Elisabeth B. MacDougall and Richard Ettinghausen, eds. *The Islamic Garden*. Dumbarton Oaks Colloquium on the History of Landscape Architecture: Harvard University Press, 1976. The introduction and five papers in this interesting volume demonstrate the wide influence of the Persian garden in literature and mysticism, as well as actual gardens.

Donald N. Wilber. *Persian Gardens and Pavilions*. Rutland, Vermont and Tokyo: Charles E. Tuttle Co., 1962. Excellent description of modern, as well as remaining old gardens with plans drawn by the author.

A Survey of Persian Art. Vol. 3. London: 1938–1939, pp. 1427–1445. An article by Arthur U. Pope and Phyllis Ackerman on Persian gardens; in addition, there are references to the Persian garden throughout the six-volume series. (Reissued in thirteen volumes in 1967.)

A. J. Arberry, ed. *Legacy of Persia*. See chapter on "The Persian Garden," by Victoria Sackville-West. Oxford: 1952.

Sylvia Crowe; Sheila Haywood; Susan Jellicoe; and Gordon Patterson. *The Gardens of Mughal India*. London: 1972. A good guide to the surviving gardens in India, profusely and beautifully illustrated.

Constance M. Villiers Stuart. *Gardens of the Great Mughals*. London: 1913. A charming account of the author's travels, impressions, of the gardens and their history. Includes watercolors by the author.

Marg, A Magazine of the Arts, Vol. 26. Bombay: December, 1972. A well-organized and illustrated issue devoted to the gardens of the Mughals.

Marie Gotheim. *History of Garden Art*. 2 Vols. Hacker Books: 1913.

Of Special Interest

Alice M. Coats. *The Quest for Plants; A History of the Horticultural Explorers.* London: 1969. An interesting bibliography of the pioneer plant-hunters.

John H. Harvey. "Turkey as a Source of Garden Plants." *Garden History: The Journal of the Garden History Society.* Vol. 6, no. 3, Autumn 1976. Excellent appendix of plants cultivated in Iran and Turkey by *ca.* 1600 A.D., including those mentioned in the *Babur-Nama*.

The following works have few references of any kind to gardens, but have excellent annotated bibliographies which evaluate source material for different periods and countries referred to in this text:

Persia and the Ancient World

Henri Frankfort. *The Art and Architecture of the Ancient Orient.* Penguin Classics, 1970. Bibliographic notes are in this revised edition.

Richard N. Frye. *Iran.* London: 1960. This work has a general annotated bibliography.

_____.*Heritage of Persia*. Cleveland: 1963. Covering the period from the Achaemenids to the late Sassanians, this work has useful notes and maps as well.

G. N. Curzon. *Persia and the Persian Question.* London: 1892. In his introduction, the author evaluates the journals of many earlier travelers.

Afghanistan

Donald N. Wilber. *Annotated Bibliography of Afghanistan*. New Haven: 1968. An excellent listing.

Nancy Hatch Dupree. *An Historical Guide to Afghanistan*. Kabul: 1971. A more select bibliography.

India

Romila Thapar. *A History of India*. Vol. 1. Penguin Classics, 1966. An excellent collection of bibliographic notes from Ancient India to the coming of the Mughals.

Percival Spear. *A History of India*. Vol. 2. Penguin Classics, 1972. Covers Indian history from the Mughals to 1965.

Benjamin Rowland. *The Art and Architecture of India, Buddhist, Hindu, Jain*. Penguin, 1970. An extensive bibliography with useful notes.

Bamber Gascoigne. *The Great Moghuls*. New York: Harper & Row, 1971. Annotated bibliography, includes notes on translations of Turki and Persian sources and an excellent select, well-arranged general listing.

Ananda K. Coomaraswamy. *Bibliographies of Indian Art*. Boston: 1925.

General Reference

Cambridge History of Iran, and Cambridge History of India. Cambridge Ancient History.
Reports of the Archaeological Survey of India, particularly the Northern Circle.
Henry Yule, and William Cooke. *Hobson-Jobson*. New Delhi: 1968. Originally published in 1903, this wonderful book is "a glossary of colloquial Anglo-Indian words and phrases, and of kindred terms, etymological, historical, geographical and discursive."
* Note the above list and notes throughout the text are available in English.

SOURCES OF ILLUSTRATIONS

Picture Credits

Pp. 15, 16, 18 (left and right), 22 (left), 26, 27, 55, 58, 59, 61, 62, 63, 64, 65, 67, 76, 77, 82, 94, 104 (left and right), 105 (left and right), 106, 107 (left and right), 117, 121, 124, 127, 129, 138, 140, 143, 144, 145, Elizabeth B. Moynihan; pp. 9, 95 (top and bottom), 113 (top), 116, 136, 137 (bottom), John Moynihan; p. 22 (right), Sylvia Matheson from *Persia, an Archaeological Guide* by Sylvia Matheson, London: Faber and Faber, 1976; p. 85, L. Bruce Laingen; p. 86, Bruce Ehrman; p. 90 (left and right), Jean Louis Nou, courtesy of Smeets Lithographers, Weert, Holland; p. 92, Walter Rawlings, from *Art and Architecture of India* by Benjamin Rowland, London: Penguin, 1967; p. 99, Christina Gascoigne; pp. 103, 114, 118, Harmit Singh.

Illustrations

Borders by Bobbi Angell
Maps by Karin H. Baker

P. 8, Bobbi Angell, after seal impressions in the Louvre; p. 17, from *Pasargadae* by David Stronach, London: Oxford University Press, 1978; p. 32, from *Paradisus Terrestris* by Lars Ivor Ringbom, Helsinki: Acta Societatis Seientiarum enicae, 1958; p. 44, from *Erste Vorlaüfer Bericht über die Ausgrabungen von Samarra* by E. Herzfeld, Berlin: Dietrich Reimer Verlag, 1912; p. 91, from *Art and Architecture of India* by Benjamin Rowland, London: Penguin, 1967; p. 133, from *The Immortal Taj Mahal* by R. Nath, Bombay: B. B. Taraporevala Sons and Co. Private Ltd., 1972; p. 137 (center), Bobbi Angell.

Index